WRONG
WINNER

WRONG WINNER

The Coming Debacle in the Electoral College

David W. Abbott
and
James P. Levine

PRAEGER

New York
Westport, Connecticut
London

Library of Congress Cataloging-in-Publication Data

Abbott, David W., 1936–
    Wrong winner : the coming debacle in the electoral college / David
W. Abbott and James P. Levine.
        p.   cm.
    Includes bibliographical references and index.
    ISBN 0–275–93780–1 (alk. paper).—ISBN 0–275–93871–9 (pbk. :
alk. paper)
    1. Electoral college—United States.   2. Presidents—United
States—Election.   I. Levine, James P.   II. Title.
JK529.A57   1991
324.6′3—dc20   90–49220

British Library Cataloguing in Publication Data is available.

Library of Congress Catalog Card Number: 90–49220
ISBN: 0–275–93780–1 (hb.)
        0–275–93871–9 (pbk.)

First published in 1991

Praeger Publishers, One Madison Avenue, New York, NY   10010
An imprint of Greenwood Publishing Group, Inc.

Printed in the United States of America

The paper used in this book complies with the
Permanent Paper Standard issued by the National
Information Standards Organization (Z39.48–1984).

10 9 8 7 6 5 4 3 2 1

To
my parents

—David W. Abbott

To
my mother and the memory of my father

—James P. Levine

Contents

Tables

Preface

There is an ominous prediction embedded in the title of this book: In the not very distant future the candidate who loses at the polls will become president of the United States. He or she will be a "wrong winner," the choice of the official electoral college but the runner-up in the popular vote. Although a century has elapsed since such a debacle has occurred, we have had many "near-misses," and it is our thesis that we are on the verge of witnessing another such spectacle. But this time the results will be far more dire than when the voters' choice was undone in 1824, 1876, and 1888. We will be confronted with a full-fledged constitutional crisis.

This, then, is a book about the complex machinery that the United States uses for selecting the president. We examine constitutional provisions, election history, and contemporary politics to reveal the shortcomings of the electoral college. Not only is there the ever-present danger of a "wrong winner," but we also show that there is a looming possibility of a "no winner" situation in which no candidate gets a majority of electoral votes and the selection of the president is shunted to the House of Representatives, where outcomes are highly unpredictable. On top of these infirmities, our analysis reveals that the current system gives some voters more power than others and frequently results in misinterpretations of the election results. We thus demonstrate that the use of the electoral college runs contrary to principles of democratic government.

The origin of this book can be traced to a precise date: November 9, 1988—the day after the election in which George Bush beat Michael Dukakis to become forty-first president of the United States. The two of us converged on our offices for the post mortems in which political scientists traditionally engage. We discovered that we had independently come up with the same insight (barely mentioned the night before by the television reporters): Dukakis had been within striking distance of winning the 270 electoral votes that would have made him president, despite having been beaten decisively in the popular vote. A third colleague joined us, glanced at the state-by-state returns in the *New York Times*, and agreed that the "time bomb" ensconced in our presidential election method could well have gone off in 1988. The study leading to this book was thus hatched: The three of us decided to investigate the strange workings of the electoral college—in the past, the present, and the future.

The third colleague was Robert Abrams. It was his computer savvy that enabled us to go to work with dispatch. We quickly put the state-by-state returns of the 1988 election and other recent elections into the computer and were able to discover just how close we had come to "wrong winner" outcomes in quite a few elections, including 1988. Abrams had to withdraw from this project to pursue other professional interests, but we acknowledge our gratitude to him for his help with the data analysis and for the steady stream of insights which he offered as we "crunched numbers" over the next few months in an attempt to figure out the peculiarities of our electoral process.

One minor problem we confronted had to do with the particular years in which we were doing our research and writing this book. Much of our analysis examines elections that have already occurred for which we have complete electoral data. However, as we speculate about the near future we do not have available to us the final results of the 1990 census upon which the electoral college vote apportionment will be based. We have therefore had to rely on preliminary Census Bureau estimates in calculating states' electoral votes for the 1990s.

We would like to thank Professor William C. Mitchell who reviewed the manuscript and made some important suggestions. Professors Steven London and Edward Rogowsky gave us the benefit of their judgment on certain important points. Mary Glenn of Praeger and Philippa Strum deserve our thanks for their early encouragement of the entire project. Thanks are also owed to Mary LaMorte for carefully word-processing the tables.

Many colleagues, friends, relatives, and students have cheerfully listened to our theories about the electoral college at times when they may have preferred to be talking about the pennant race, good restaurants, or the latest movies. Their willingness to ask tough questions helped us clarify our thinking and our explanations. We thank them all.

POSTSCRIPT

A final draft of WRONG WINNER had already been submitted when Iraq invaded Kuwait. Minor modifications were made to reflect the Persian Gulf events of early January 1991. Now the authors sit glued to CNN news reports of the ground war that has just begun. It appears that a massive allied victory is imminent, with very low casualties. Although we cannot know how events will unfold, it seems probable that the war will bolster President Bush's already high political standing, making the closely contested election envisioned in Chapter 1's scenario unlikely. The new facts of the Persian Gulf war do not in any way invalidate the point illustrated by our hypothetical 1992 scenario—that the electoral college mechanism will soon misfire and produce a "wrong winner."

1

The Coming Constitutional Crisis

THE DEBACLE OF 1996

It finally happened. Scientists had been issuing warnings about it for years but the politicians and business leaders and media people had not taken the warnings very seriously. There had been occasional references to the danger in newspaper columns and on the Sunday morning interview shows, but nobody seemed very worried about it. And, of course, it happened in California.

The Great San Andreas earthquake? No. Scientists had been predicting that for years, too. There had been lots of warnings. The 1989 Bay Area quake was only the most dramatic indication that "the Big One" was coming. But, in spite of all the warnings, not much was done to avoid the consequences that would finally occur.

But, *this* disaster had been predicted by *political* scientists, not geologists. The last time such an event had occurred was in 1888, almost two decades before the great San Francisco earthquake of 1906. And, like the great California quake, experts knew that we were due for another one. In 1992, the cumbersome and quirky electoral machinery that the Founders had improvised two centuries earlier finally misfired again, the first such breakdown in the twentieth century, the first time it had happened in the age of mass media democracy. In 1996, the electoral college had selected *the wrong president*!

It had been a hard-fought campaign; the polls had shown a close race ever since the Republican convention in August. As usual, the Republican ticket was ahead in the polls but, for the first time in years, the Democratic nominee had strong enough public appeal to hold the Republicans to a narrow lead.

Bill Bradley had entered the traditionally crowded Democratic field rather late, but had been gaining in stature and popularity almost continuously since. His speaking style had improved considerably and he had gotten over the "woodenness" that had characterized his career earlier. The numerous Democratic candidate debates in late 1995 and early 1996 had gone well for him. Following the pattern of Carter in 1976 and Dukakis in 1988, he managed to establish a lead in the early caucuses and primaries and never fell behind. But, unlike previous Democratic front-runners, Bradley was seen as clearly "presidential" and fully qualified. Blue-collar Democrats, so often turned off by their national party's conventions, were hanging in this time, and not simply because they liked the former professional basketball star who was their nominee. Euphoria about the smashing American victory over Iraq which had so benefited Republican fortunes in the election of 1992 had long since dissipated, and the nation was having to come to grips with the huge backlog of critical domestic problems which had barely been addressed during the Reagan/Bush years. Poverty and homelessness, the crumbling cities, the decaying infrastructure, educational and health system reform, energy conservation and environmental degradation had moved onto center stage to the advantage of the Democrats who traditionally are more concerned with these kinds of issues. The polls showed that blacks seemed pleased with Bradley's candidacy, while Jewish voters and union members appeared to be returning to the Democratic fold.

Of course, part of Bradley's strength was a function of his opponent's relative weakness. Dan Quayle was the most ineffective Republican candidate since Gerald Ford. Not that he had run such a bad campaign. Quayle had grown in stature considerably in his eight years as vice president. His boyish good looks had improved with age and he now "looked like a president," in the manner of a Jack Kennedy. But he had never been able to shake the impression that he wasn't really very smart, that there was less there than met the eye. The debates had not been a disaster for him—in fact, because of the requirement that the questions be submitted twenty-four hours in advance, he had not made any major missteps. But, most of the commentators agreed that Bradley, the former Rhodes scholar, had "won" both of them. Quayle's greatest strength was that he was a Republican. The Republican Party had dominated presidential elections for the last thirty years. The political realignment in the South in the 1960s had produced a new "Solid South" that was overwhelmingly Republican in presidential elections (and increasingly Republican in state and local races, as well). In 1991, the Gallup Poll had begun to show the Republicans coming abreast of the Democrats and even moving ahead of them in party identification, the first time that had happened since 1940. By September 1996 the Gallup Poll had the Republicans with a three-point party identification advantage: Republican 41 percent, Democrat 38 percent, Independent 21 percent. Given the traditionally lower voter turnout among Democrats, the real Republican advantage was even greater than the three-point spread suggested.

But in spite of this shrinkage in their political base, Democrats had continued to show strength in Congress, in part because of the favorable apportionment they got from the mostly Democratic legislatures in 1991 and in part because of the continuing advantages of incumbency for House members. Although their majority in the House of Representatives had been trimmed considerably since 1992, they still dominated in the urban areas and maintained considerable strength in suburban districts in the Northeast, the industrial Midwest, and in an increasing number of districts around the country, sometimes referred to in the press as "Green Country," where environmental concerns had moved to the forefront.

In spite of the closeness of the contest, all the polls were showing Republican Quayle leading his Democratic opponent by four or five points. He had the very large leads in the South and in most of the "big square states" in the West that we had come to associate with Republican candidates like Nixon, Reagan, and Bush. But various newspaper polls conducted in individual states showed Bradley even or slightly ahead in many of the big electoral states that Republicans had been carrying in recent years—states like Illinois, Ohio, Michigan, California, and Missouri. And, of course, he had a big lead in his home state, normally-Republican New Jersey, and was comfortably ahead in neighboring New York and Pennsylvania.

In early October a handful of newspaper stories began to mention the possibility that Vice President Quayle, because of his huge leads in the South, the Southwest, and the Mountain States might succeed in winning a majority of the popular vote but fall short of the necessary majority of the electoral college vote. According to these analyses, the outcome would hinge on the results in California, which the polls were showing "too close to call."

And California was close—Democrat Bradley carried the Golden State by a razor-thin margin of 192,000 votes out of a total of over 10 million cast! But that was enough. With California's 54 electors, Bradley's electoral college vote passed the magic 270 mark, assuring him victory. And this in spite of the fact that Dan Quayle had won a clear majority of the popular votes cast, a majority of almost 2 million votes! (See Table 1.1.)

A fantastic scenario? Sure it is. Far-fetched? Not at all. But this exercise in crystal ball-gazing is not designed to forecast the names and prospects of the presidential candidates in 1996. That would be a risky business, indeed, given the strange twists and turns in political events over a six year period of time. Our purpose, rather, is to illustrate the danger of a presidential candidate's winning the presidency despite having lost the popular vote to the other party. In the scenario we sketched out above, the beneficiary was Bill Bradley. But it could just as easily be Al Gore of Tennessee, Mario Cuomo of New York, Sam Nunn of Georgia, or even a long shot like Bob Kerrey of Nebraska. It is our contention that in any presidential election in the foreseeable future where the Democratic popular vote loser comes within a percentage point or two of the Republican candidate, the Democrat will win the electoral college and the presidency.

We don't know the actual cast of characters but this much is certain: The electoral college is going to choose a "wrong winner" some time in the near future.

But that is not the only irrationality inherent in our electoral system. In addition to possibly picking the wrong winner, the electoral college also:

1. poses the threat of a full-blown, paralyzing constitutional crisis if a presidential election were to be thrown into the House of Representatives.

2. encourages third party "spoilers";

3. gives extraordinary political weight to the votes of some states and some groups and denies other voters their fair share of influence, egregiously violating the principle of "one person, one vote";

4. drastically distorts the nature and implications of the voters' decisions and creates "false mandates;"

5. contributes to low voter turnout and acts to reinforce one-partyism in the states;

6. poses a real threat to the election of any Republican presidential nominee in a close election.

In this book, we will describe and illustrate all of these phenomena. But first, we must go back a couple of centuries to discern how our strange system of electing a president came into being. As we shall now see, the electoral college system with its potential for producing "wrong winners" has deeply embedded constitutional and historical roots.

Table 1.1
Hypothetical 1996 Presidential Vote

State	Electoral Votes*		Popular Votes	
	Quayle	Bradley	Quayle	Bradley
Alabama	9		809,663	687,347
Alaska	3		102,381	78,205
Arizona	8		701,379	467,272
Arkansas	6		473,574	364,991
California		54	5,006,490	5,098,393
Colorado	8		727,633	651,093
Connecticut		8	707,082	734,873
Delaware	3		130,581	101,479
District of Columbia		3	25,732	175,123
Florida	25		2,568,994	1,745,086
Georgia	13		1,070,089	915,635
Hawaii		4	178,625	205,364
Idaho	4		253,467	157,420
Illinois		22	2,198,648	2,380,657
Indiana	12		1,280,292	940,851
Iowa		7	501,540	538,095
Kansas	6		552,659	435,056
Kentucky	8		721,446	609,077
Louisiana	9		850,830	765,612
Maine	4		301,087	255,508

6

Maryland	10		804,939	845,939
Massachusetts	12		1,264,323	1,406,398
Michigan	18		1,801,434	1,873,496
Minnesota	10		958,296	1,144,975
Mississippi		7	541,745	374,982
Missouri	11		1,005,024	1,159,146
Montana		3	179,598	166,120
Nebraska		5	379,394	254,426
Nevada		4	255,942	133,716
New Hampshire		4	299,770	178,335
New Jersey	15		1,340,063	1,661,634
New Mexico		5	290,762	266,528
New York	33		2,802,276	3,378,904
North Carolina		14	1,232,132	990,034
North Dakota		3	165,517	147,081
Ohio	21		2,134,922	2,234,719
Oklahoma		8	658,244	533,373
Oregon	7		507,731	598,071
Pennsylvania	23		2,082,983	2,391,298
Rhode Island	4		169,989	226,271
South Carolina		8	575,871	389,511
South Dakota		3	160,516	155,632
Tennessee		11	939,434	685,715
Texas		32	3,008,007	2,531,286

Table 1.1 (continued)

State	Electoral Votes*		Popular Votes	
	Quayle	Bradley	Quayle	Bradley
Utah	5		416,868	226,913
Vermont		3	101,166	131,419
Virginia	13		1,305,131	960,767
Washington		11	789,182	874,554
West Virginia		5	308,824	339,112
Wisconsin		11	1,042,584	1,332,090
Wyoming	3		116,854	77,007
	246	292	46,791,713	44,976,589

* The apportionment of electoral votes to the states is based on preliminary Census Bureau estimates released in August, 1990, as reported in *The New York Times*, August 29, 1990.

A BRIEF HISTORY OF THE ELECTORAL COLLEGE

When the Framers gathered in Philadelphia in 1787, they were intent on strengthening the capabilities of their fledgling government. In the course of that extraordinary summer they came to agree upon the idea of a chief magistrate, a president, to exercise the executive power. This was a major decision and a very significant change; the Articles of Confederation had made no provision for a single executive authority. No member present doubted that George Washington would be the first president if their new constitution were approved by the states. There was, however, considerable disagreement about the mechanism for selecting the chief executive. Simplicity and logic led one faction to favor selection of the president by Congress. It was a familiar arrangement—at the time, the governors of most of the states were selected by their legislatures. Moreover, presidential selection by Congress presented none of the logistical problems that would be inherent in direct election by the people. But opponents of congressional selection of the president argued persuasively that a president chosen by Congress would be politically beholden to the legislature, a "mere creature" of that body. They were concerned that the presidency would be weakened and compromised by its dependency on the legislative branch.

The obvious alternative to selection of the chief executive by the Congress was to have him elected by the people. Although direct election was favored by some of the most prominent members of the convention, including Madison, it did not have the support of more than a few members. The two times the direct vote alternative was presented to the convention, it was overwhelmingly defeated. Supporters of direct election saw it as a way of guaranteeing the independence of the president from the Congress and protecting the people from legislative tyranny. Most members, however, felt that the general public was ill prepared for such momentous responsibility. Hamilton was somewhat more blunt. "Your people, sir, are a great beast!" he exclaimed during a debate on the merits of popular election. And, although not recorded as part of the discussion, the practical difficulties and expense of a national presidential election also militated against such a procedure at that time.

In spite of the failure of advocates of direct election to win approval of their plan, they apparently were able to cast sufficient doubt on the wisdom of having the chief executive selected by Congress to open the way for a compromise proposal, a separate body of electors, chosen in the states, that would be empowered to elect the president independent of Congress.

It has been argued that the electoral college scheme was less a product of wisdom and philosophy than the result of a practical compromise.[1] The provision for an electoral college struck a sort of balance between congressional selection and selection by some state-based process. Since everyone knew that Washington would be the first president in any case, no matter what method was decided upon, and since each of the other alternatives was fraught with problems, the electoral college compromise, while lacking any intrinsic virtue, at least had the advantage of commanding a majority of the convention, allowing the question to be gotten off the table and done with. The future could take care of itself.

So the compromise was struck. It provided that:

> Each state shall appoint, in such manner as the legislature thereof may direct, a number of electors, equal to the whole number of Senators and Representatives to which the state may be entitled in Congress,

thus giving all states a base electoral vote of three, with additional votes assigned to larger states on the basis of their populations.

All electors were to meet on the same day in their respective states and vote for two persons for president, at least one of whom was not to be from their own state. A list of all persons who received presidential votes, and the number of votes each received, was to be sent to the national capital, directed to the president of the Senate. There, on an appointed day, the ballots were to be opened and announced at a joint session of Congress. The candidate having the greatest number of electoral votes, if that number was an absolute majority of the total electoral college, would be declared president. The runner-up would be vice president. If no candidate received a majority of the electoral votes, the House of Representatives was to select the president from among the five candidates who had received the most electoral votes, the House voting by states, with each state having one vote. A majority of all the states would be necessary for election. The runner-up would be vice president. In 1796, of the sixteen states, six allowed the voters to elect presidential electors directly. In the remaining ten states, the electors were chosen by the state legislatures.

We can only imagine what the Framers expected of this jerry-built contraption. It is safe to say that they assumed that George Washington would receive an automatic majority of the electoral college in the first election and, perhaps, in the second and even the third election as well. After Washington, they may have imagined that most presidential elections would be resolved in Congress, from among candidates nominated by electors in the states, on the assumption that normally no one would receive a majority of electoral votes. The electoral college members, then, would act as nominators, proposing the five names from among whom the House of Representatives, voting by state, would select the president.

The Framers' predictions of a sure Washington victory were fully justified—in the first two elections, Washington received *every* elector's vote! It was in the succeeding election that the Framers' expectations were not met.

What the Framers hadn't counted on was the emergence of national political parties. Serious divisions had begun to appear during Washington's first administration. The central characters in the factional struggles were Hamilton and Jefferson, both members of the cabinet. So serious were their differences that Jefferson had offered to resign, but Washington preferred to keep him in the government in the interest of national unity (and perhaps to prevent him from causing even more trouble *outside* the government).

The administration became a de facto coalition government. The rival secretaries continued to work against each other and to organize their respective supporters in the Congress, as well as in the states. The followers of Jefferson and his close ally and confidant, Madison, became known as Republicans (later to become the Democratic-Republicans and then, simply, the Democrats). Hamilton's party became known as the Federalists.

In 1796, President Washington announced that he would not seek a third term, setting a precedent for a two-term presidency that would go unchallenged for almost 150 years. The Federalist members of Congress caucused that summer and nominated Vice President John Adams of Massachusetts for president and Thomas Pinckney of South Carolina for vice president. The Republican congressional caucus selected Thomas Jefferson of Virginia for president and Aaron Burr of New York for vice president.

In its first independent operation, then, it became obvious that the electoral college would not be the dispassionate body the Framers had apparently envisaged, conscientiously seeking out the best-qualified person for the chief magistrate's position. Nor would it be simply a nominating body, suggesting names of potential presidential candidates to the House of Representatives for its consideration. Instead, the electors were to become pawns in a larger partisan game, acting as agents of their respective political parties to elect their party's standard bearer president. The events of 1796 made it clear that the nominating function was to be removed from the electors and taken over by the parties' congressional caucuses, and that the processes of selection of the electors in the states would be dominated by partisan, not personal, considerations.

Washington's decision to retire threw the Federalist Party into disarray. Lacking its central unifying figure, the party was torn by personal and regional rivalries that showed up in the contests for presidential electors and the votes they cast. Hamilton and many of the southern Federalists did not like Adams. Many New Englanders, on the other hand, refused to support Pinckney. The result was a near-disaster for the Federalists. Federalists won a majority of the seats in the electoral college, but when the electors met in their respective states, some of the Pinckney supporters refused to vote for Adams and even more of the Adams men refused to cast their electoral votes for Pinckney. The result was that, although Adams was elected President, Pinckney was edged out of second place (the vice presidency) by Thomas Jefferson, the *Republican* presidential nominee!

Since the emergence of the two parties, it had become clear that there would be two leading candidates for president and that the "double balloting" system (where each elector cast *two* votes for president) would create problems. These problems had been recognized almost from the beginning, but it was not until 1796 that the system "misfired," producing unintended results by selecting the "wrong" vice president. The double-balloting system would cause even more trouble four years later.

In the election of 1800, the Federalist caucus re-nominated the incumbent, Adams, for president and named C. C. Pinckney of South Carolina, the brother of Thomas Pinckney, as his running mate. The Republicans once more nominated Jefferson for president and Burr for vice president. It was a close and bitter contest marked by public charges and behind-the-scenes manipulations. In the end, Jefferson's Republicans carried the day, out-polling the Federalists in the electoral vote by a margin of only eight votes. But each of the Republican electors was to cast *two* votes. In order to avoid a tie while also preventing the kind of mixed outcome that had occurred in the previous election, Republican leaders had intended to have one of their electors refrain from giving Burr his vote. But, because of a misunderstanding or, perhaps, because of some secret move by Burr, the plan broke down; both Jefferson and Burr received 73 electoral votes. Jefferson found himself in a tie with his vice presidential running mate![2]

Since neither had a majority, the election, according to constitutional provision, was thrown into the House, where each state delegation would cast a single vote. However, the Federalists dominated most of the state delegations in the House. Therefore, the final decision as to which of their opponents would become president would be up to them. For weeks during the winter of 1800–1801 the House went through thirty-five ballots. Some Federalists hoped to make new arrangements for presidential succession so that a Federalist might be selected. Others, fearing civil unrest if no election were made, advocated reaching some accommodation with Burr and electing him. Sill others, including Hamilton, mistrusted Burr so deeply that they preferred even the hated Jefferson. Finally, after weeks of political maneuvering, on the thirty-sixth ballot, Federalist representatives from several states cast blank ballots, and another absented himself, thus tipping their states' votes to Jefferson, thereby giving him a majority of the states, and the election. The runner-up, Burr, was declared vice president.

The election of 1800 had vividly demonstrated the weakness of the double-ballot system in the electoral college. Not only could it create a tie between the winning party's presidential and vice presidential candidates, as it had in 1800, it could produce a president of one party and a vice president of another, as it had in 1796. It could also allow the losing party's electors to make mischief by switching their votes to the other party's *vice* presidential candidate, thereby electing *him*, rather than his party's presidential nominee, president.

Demands for constitutional revision of the double-balloting provision were widespread. By 1803, five states' legislatures had gone on record as favoring revision. Late in that year Congress passed the Twelfth Amendment and sent it to the states for approval. By the following September it had been ratified, just in time for the election of 1804. The amendment provided for separate ballots for president and vice president, required absolute majorities of the electoral college for each office, and provided for contingent election of vice president by the Senate.

Thus, by 1804, the basic outlines of the current electoral college system were nearly complete. Only one further detail remained unresolved—the method of selection of the electors.

As we noted above, the Philadelphia constitution had left the method of selection of electors to the legislatures of the respective states. In the first several elections, the most common arrangement was for the legislatures to select the electors themselves. However, by 1800, over half of the states featured selection systems that gave the voters at least a partial role in choosing electors. But there was not going to be an immediate rush to popular selection of electors. For the next couple of decades states' systems would be in flux, often shifting with the imperatives of anticipated partisan advantage. However, demands for democracy were widespread and insistent, and by 1832 direct election had been adopted in all but one of the states. The last holdout, South Carolina, did not go to popular election until after the Civil War.

Some of the states that did adopt popular election plans provided for district-by-district selection, usually with statewide at-large election or legislative selection of the two "senatorial" electors. Other states went immediately to the at-large or general ticket system whereby all electors would be elected by the state's voters on a single slate. The general ticket system was widely preferred by states' dominant political factions because of its "winner-take-all" quality. Whereas under the district system it was often necessary to divide the state's electoral vote between the two parties, under a general ticket system the dominant party could nullify the votes of the minority and deliver a solid bloc of electors to their party's national ticket, thereby buttressing its claims for patronage and other rewards from the new administration. This unit rule system also gave greater weight to the states that used it than to states whose votes were divided under a district system, providing further incentive for those district system states to switch to a general ticket, winner-take-all system. The political logic and competitive pressure from other states became irresistible. One state followed another in switching to a winner-take-all system. By 1836 virtually every state had adopted it. Although there were attempts to amend the Constitution to require a return to the more "democratic" district system of election, they were overwhelmed by the persuasiveness of partisan advantage, political self-interest, and state power.

Thus it was that the current electoral college system took its final form, not by constitutional amendment but by the actions of state legislatures. With the final addition of the recalcitrant South Carolina in 1868, all of the states would have their electors chosen by statewide electorates and all would cast their presidential ballots in unit blocs, winner-take-all. (There have been two exceptions since . . . First, Michigan had a brief flirtation with the district system in 1892. As a result, Michigan's electoral votes were divided between the two parties that year. Second, in recent years, Maine has operated under the district system. However, Maine has only two congressional districts and they have never had divergent presidential outcomes, so the pattern of unified state voting has been the rule in this century, except for a scattering of "faithless electors" who cast maverick ballots without affecting presidential outcomes.)

THE PRESENT ELECTORAL COLLEGE
SYSTEM

The methods of presidential nomination and the style of election campaigns have been transformed repeatedly since the 1820s. The congressional caucus method of nomination yielded in the 1830s to national party nominating conventions, which continue, at least in form, to this day. However, since the 1960s, the nominating function of the national conventions has largely been shifted to the mass media and a series of primaries and open state convention systems where presidential candidates seek public support in the delegate selection process that precedes the conventions. The conventions themselves have become mere ratifying bodies for decisions that were made earlier.[3]

Presidential general election campaigns have also been transformed by the decline of party organization, the rise of television, and the growth of public affluence and education. Media managers and campaign consultants, receiving guidance from opinion pollsters, produce candidates who speak in "sound bites" and give photo opportunities.

But, amidst all of these changes, the electoral college has remained more or less constant in its operations, if not in its political effects. How does it work?

First of all, the electoral college is organized state by state. Each state is allotted, under the Constitution, a number of electors "equal to the whole number of Senators and Representatives to which the state may be entitled in Congress." In 1961, the Twenty-Third Amendment awarded three electors to the District of Columbia, bringing the total number of electors to 538. Following the constitutional pattern of apportionment of the Congress, each state is awarded a minimum of three electors, since each state is guaranteed two senators and at least one representative. And since the constitution requires a reapportionment of the House of Representatives every ten years, following each decennial census, the electoral college is automatically reapportioned each decade to reflect shifts in population from state to state. For example, as the result of the 1990 census, California's electoral vote went from 47 to 54 while New York's dropped from 36 to *33* reflecting national population shifts in course of the previous ten years.

Each state, then, is assigned a given number of "seats" or votes in the electoral college. But what is the process by which these seats are filled? The particulars vary from state to state; the following is a general description of the process. State law provides that a designated party organ, most frequently a state party convention or a state party central committee, occasionally a party primary, names a slate of elector candidates equal in number to the state's senators and representatives. These party organs usually meet and make their selections of elector slates in the weeks immediately following the national party convention. Typically, the people designated as elector candidates are party stalwarts known for their faithful service and for their loyalty.

Only rarely are they characters of giant ego or burning ambition; their designation is seen as an honor and rewarded for faithful party service, a plaque or certificate to hang on the den wall. These are not the kinds of people who are likely to go off on their own and cast a presidential ballot for anyone other than their party's official nominee, to whom they are pledged (and, in some states, legally bound).

Having been duly nominated by the appropriate party body, the elector candidates' names are then submitted to the state's secretary of state for certification as the party's official slate of elector candidates. Each state has legal provision for the selection and certification of third-party slates of elector candidates as well, although these processes are often cumbersome.

In most states the names of the elector candidates no longer appear on the ballot, and in virtually all of the states the voter casts a single vote for the whole slate rather than voting separately for the individual electors. Voters may not even realize that they are voting for elector slates rather than for presidential candidates directly. For instance, voters looking at the ballot in a voting machine might cast their presidential votes by pulling a switch labeled, in very small letters, "Electors For" and, in very large letters, "GEORGE BUSH." Whether they know it or not, those voters are not voting directly for George Bush but, rather, are casting one vote for each person on the Republican slate of electors in that state, all of whom are pledged to vote for George *if their slate wins*, that is, if George Bush carries the state. And this is how the winner-take-all result occurs. If a plurality of the state's voters prefer Bush, their votes actually elect the *whole slate* of Republican electors, giving him *all* of the state's electoral votes, regardless of the closeness of the popular vote.

The voters choose the electors on election day, and by that evening the television networks have announced the results in all but the closest contests and have usually projected the presidential winner by 10 P.M. Eastern Time. However, the *actual* presidential election won't occur until the following month, when the electors of all of the states and the District of Columbia meet in their respective state capitals to mark formally their ballots for president and vice president. (It is at this point, some five weeks after the popular votes were cast and the election results became known, that an occasional elector, usually from the losing party, knowing that the electoral outcome is a foregone conclusion, casts his or her ballot for some symbolic candidate other than the nominee of that elector's party.) Once the electors have cast their formal ballots in their respective state capitals, the ballots are forwarded to the president of the Senate in Washington, D.C. There, in early January, the president of the Senate (the incumbent vice president of the United States), before a joint session of Congress, formally announces the electoral votes of each state and declares the winner. In January 1989, Vice President George Bush had the pleasure of certifying his own election as president.

It is this complicated set of procedures and the consequences that derive from them that are the subject of this book. The authors at first intended to call the book *The Founders' Folly*. The provision for selecting the chief executive has proved to be one of the most defective features of the Constitution of 1787. And, after two hundred years, the problems have still not been resolved. Early in the chapter, we named seven major negative consequences of the electoral college system of presidential selection. It is to these negative consequences and their remedies that this book is addressed. The first and most extraordinary of these is that the electoral college can select "*the wrong winner*"!

NOTES

1. John P. Roche, "The Founding Fathers: A Reform Caucus in Action" *American Political Science Review* (December 1961), pp. 799–816.

2. For a more thorough discussion of the historical development of the electoral college, see Neal R. Peirce and Lawrence D. Longley, *The People's President: The Electoral College in American History and the Direct Vote Alternative*, rev. ed. (New Haven, Conn.: Yale University Press, 1981), chaps. 2 and 3.

3. Byron E. Shafer, *Bifurcated Politics: Evolution and Reform in the National Party Convention* (Cambridge, Mass.: Harvard University Press, 1988), pp. 17–25.

2

Wrong Winners

Of all of the features of the electoral college that make it controversial, none is as significant as the built-in possibility of a "wrong winner," where the popular vote loser manages to win the electoral college majority and the presidency. It happened last in 1888, when Grover Cleveland received 95,000 more votes than Benjamin Harrison but lost the presidency. Cleveland's victory among the voters was not enough; Harrison won where it counted—in the electoral college.

In this chapter we shall see that Harrison's second-place victory was no fluke; we will find that the specter of a "wrong winner" outcome looms continuously over our presidential elections. First, we will explain how such events can occur—the mechanisms and circumstances that make it possible for the popular vote and electoral vote to diverge. Then we will discuss the few instances where it has actually occurred and the many other occasions when it almost happened. We will show how "wrong winners" might be selected in both *very close* elections (like 1960 and 1968) and those that were *not very close* at all (like 1976 and 1988). Finally, we will describe the constitutional "time bomb" confronting the nation—the realistic *probability* of a modern-day repeat of the bizarre outcome of 1888.

HOW "WASTED VOTES" CAUSE WRONG WINNERS

The "wrong winner" possibility is a product of the state-by-state winner-take-all allocation of electoral votes. It happens like this: the popular vote runner-up (the "wrong winner") manages to *eke out narrow popular vote margins* in enough states to win a majority of the electoral college. The other, more popular candidate, while winning almost as many popular votes in those states, fails to pick up any of their electors because of the winner-take-all feature of the system. Meanwhile, the more popular candidate may have racked up enormous majorities in the remaining states. Those votes, when added to the votes cast for that candidate in the states that were lost by narrow margins, might add up to an impressive popular vote majority. Nevertheless, in spite of the voters' clear mandate, the more popular candidate will lose the election that counts—the electoral college. That loss will be the result of "wasted votes," the "extra" votes that the more popular candidate received in the states that he or she carried by landslides. Those millions of "wasted votes" produced a popular vote majority but failed to produce the crucial electoral votes that could translate popularity into election.

Let us illustrate how "wasted votes" can produce a "wrong winner" by using a real-world four-state example from the 1988 presidential election. Table 2.1 lists the actual popular and electoral vote results from four states in 1988. Imagine that these four states composed a complete nation.

Dukakis, carrying New York by a slim popular vote plurality, picked up all of New York's 36 electors. Even though Bush received over 3 million votes in the Empire State, he won no electors there. However, Bush carried the *other* three states by landslides, winning 66 percent of the vote in Utah, 60 percent in Arizona, and 62 percent in South Carolina. His plurality in those three landslide states (705, 491) was much greater than Dukakis' plurality in New York (266, 011), giving Bush a clear 52.4 percent "nationwide" majority. However, Dukakis, despite hav-

Table 2.1
"Wasted Votes" and "Wrong Winner": Four-State Example—1988

	Dukakis		Bush	
	Popular Vote	Electors	Popular Vote	Electors
New York	3,347,882	36	3,081,871	0
Utah	207,352	0	428,442	5
Arizona	454,029	0	702,541	7
South Carolina	370,554	0	606,443	8
TOTALS	4,379,817	36	4,819,297	20
	(47.6%)		(52.4%)	

ing been defeated at the polls, would *win* the presidency in our hypothetical four-state "nation" by winning the electoral college vote 36 to 20!

Another way of visualizing a "wrong winner" scenario is to imagine that the winning candidate carried the twelve largest states (and their 279 electors) by narrow 10,000 vote margins in each of those states. Thus, the winner's total plurality in those twelve states was 120,000 votes. However, our winner lost the remaining states overwhelmingly, by an average of 100,000 votes per state. The other candidate's plurality in those thirty-eight states would, therefore, be 3,800,000. Thus, although the losing candidate received 3,680,000 more votes nationwide, the other candidate would win the electoral college vote 279 to 259! The less popular candidate, who had won razor-thin victories in the twelve largest states (and who might have won *no votes whatsoever* in the remaining thirty-eight states!), would be the one moving into the White House in January.

Ultimately, any "wrong winner" scenario is based on the premise of "wasted votes." Popular winners "waste" votes in two ways. First, the votes they win in states that they *fail* to carry (e.g., the 2.9 million votes Bush won in New York in the four-state example above) are essentially "thrown away." They win no electors in such states so those votes don't do them any good in the electoral college, and they can't move those wasted votes around to other states where they could do some good. Second, they also "waste" all of the "extra" votes they receive in the states that they carry by large margins (Utah, Arizona, and South Carolina in the four-state example). They only "needed" the votes that gave them unchallengeable majorities in those states; any votes over and above that were unnecessary. They, too, were "wasted." This *inefficient* (in electoral college terms) distribution of votes can produce a "wrong winner." It isn't just *how many* votes a candidate receives, but *where* those votes are cast, that counts in the electoral college system.

WRONG WINNERS IN HISTORY

Let us go back and look at the last time the electoral college produced a "wrong winner"—1888. It was a classic example of the "wasted vote" phenomenon. The popular vote winner, the Democrat, Grover Cleveland, won eighteen states, including the "Solid South." Although Cleveland won a few of his states by narrow margins, many of the Southern states gave Cleveland popular majorities in the two-to-one, three-to-one, even five-to-one range. Cleveland's average vote in the states he won was 58.8 percent. These lopsided victories, as satisfying as they must have been, were terribly inefficient in terms of electoral votes. They included tens of thousands of "wasted votes," votes that Cleveland didn't need in those states (since he had already won their electors handily) but that he could have used elsewhere to carry some of the "cliff-hanger" states he was losing. The Republican, Benjamin Harrison, on the other hand, was winning state after state by slim pluralities in the 0 to 4 percent range (thirteen states out of his twenty). Harrison's average popular vote in the states he won was only 53.3 percent. Harrison's geographical vote distribution was much more "efficient" than Cleveland's since many fewer of his votes were being "wasted" in useless margins in states already won. So, although he trailed Cleveland by almost 100,000 votes nationwide, Harrison won the electoral college vote 233 to 168 and, thereby, the White House!

The sense of shock and popular outrage about a "wrong winner" in 1888 must have been tempered by the fact that such events were not unheard of—in fact there had been an electoral college misfire, a "wrong winner," just twelve years earlier, in 1876. In that election Democrat Samuel Tilden had a quarter-million vote plurality (and a clear majority of the votes cast) over Republican Rutherford Hayes but lost the electoral college vote and the presidency. Eight years later, in 1884, the Democratic candidate, Grover Cleveland, came within six hundred votes in one state of being defeated by another "wrong winner." Cleveland, who so narrowly avoided a "wrong winner" defeat in 1884, would not manage to escape such a fate in his bid for reelection in 1888.

Thus, in a brief period late in the last century, out of four consecutive and highly competitive presidential elections, two produced "wrong winners" and a third came within a hair's breadth of dong so.[1] During that period, the capacity of the electoral college to overrule the voters' decision was not just an academic possibility but a palpable reality.

"NEAR-MISSES" IN CLOSE ELECTIONS

The possibilities of "wrong winner" outcomes are greatest in elections where the popular vote and the electoral vote are both close.[2] As mentioned above, there was a very close call in 1884 when Grover Cleveland defeated James G. Blaine by a narrow margin in the electoral college vote (219 to 182) and in the popular vote (4,875,971 to 4,852,234). In that election, with the popular and electoral votes nearly tied, a shift of only 575 votes in New York would have given the electoral college victory to the popular vote loser. There were several other close calls. In 1892, the rematch between Benjamin Harrison and Grover Cleveland was won by Cleveland, who had a plurality of over 370,000 votes. However, a shift of less than 40,000 votes from Cleveland to Harrison would have reelected Harrison, making him a "wrong winner" yet again. In 1896, the shift of only 21,000 votes would have prevented McKinley's victory over William Jennings Bryan, in spite of his almost 600,000 vote plurality! The threat of a wrong winner hung like a dark cloud over *every election from 1876 to 1896* because of the extreme closeness of party competition in that era.

In this century there have been a number of very close elections, some of which have also featured closely divided electoral votes. One of them, the election of 1916, has received very little attention. Woodrow Wilson, running for reelection, came very close to suffering a "wrong winner" defeat. Four years earlier, Wilson had won a 42 percent plurality victory in a three-way race against a sundered majority Republican Party. In that year the Republicans, hopelessly divided by the challenge of former President Theodore Roosevelt to the renomination of incumbent President William Howard Taft, split, with Roosevelt forming the insurgent "Bull Moose Party." The minority Democrats and their standardbearer prevailed against their divided foe, winning 42 percent of the popular vote to Taft's 23 percent and Roosevelt's 27 percent. Socialist Eugene Debs got six percent. The electoral vote in 1912 was: Wilson—435, Roosevelt—88, Taft—8. No wrong-winner possibility here—the electoral vote, even though it exaggerated the size of Wilson's victory, was consistent with the popular vote outcome.

In 1916, a chastened and more-or-less reunified Republican Party nominated Charles Evans Hughes to challenge the incumbent Wilson. The popular vote was fairly close, with the president winning 49 percent to Hughes's 46 percent. The electoral vote was also close, with Wilson winning 277 to 254. California, with its 13 (!) electoral votes, had gone to Wilson by a narrow margin. A shift of only two thousand votes from Wilson to Hughes in California would have elected Hughes by an electoral vote of 267 to 264, in spite of Wilson's half-million vote nationwide plurality. Wilson, the voters' choice, would have been kicked out of the White House in the middle of the Great War in Europe, with possibly enormous consequences for world history, and all because of the electoral college's peculiar mechanism for counting the peoples' presidential votes.

If closely contested presidential contests were the norm in the late nineteenth century, they have been much less common since that time. The closest contest in this century in terms of electoral college votes, 1916, (277 to 254), was followed by 1976 (297 to 240) and 1960 (303 to 219). Two others in recent times have featured fairly strong showings by the losers: 1948 (303 to 189) and 1968 (301 to 191 to 46). Most elections in this century were electoral college landslides, with the loser often getting less than a hundred electors and outnumbered three or four or five to one in electoral votes. Such electoral college "wipe-outs" occurred in 1920, 1924, 1928, 1932, 1936, 1940, 1944, 1952, 1956, 1964, 1972, 1980, and 1984. And, in all of these "wipe-out" years, with the exception of 1980, the popular vote was also lopsided. In cases like these, wrong-winner possibilities do not exist, and, because there have been so many of these popular vote landslides (or near-landslides), there have been few opportunities for the wrong-winner outcome to occur in this century. However, whenever there is a closely contested presidential election, the threat of an electoral college debacle returns.

In fact, only four elections in this century have been very close in terms of popular votes (1948, 1960, 1968, and 1976), and each came close to producing a wrong winner.

In 1948, a shift of only 30,000 votes in three states (17,000 in Illinois, out of almost 3.9 million cast, 9,000 in California out of 3.8 million cast, and 4,000 in Ohio out of 2.9 million cast) would have delivered the White House to Governor Dewey, in spite of the fact that he trailed President Truman by some 2.1 million votes! Unlike the razor-thin margins of the 1880s, the popular vote majority in 1948 was very clear-cut. Truman led 49.5 percent to 45.1 percent (third-party candidates Strom Thurmond and Henry Wallace got most of the remaining votes). But, because of some very close contests in a few big states and a relatively balanced electoral vote, the system came close to producing a wrong winner.

In 1960, we had a slightly different situation. In that election, the popular vote was essentially tied, as it was in 1884. The official tally read:

> Kennedy—34,221,344
> Nixon—34,106,671

Allegations of voting irregularities in Illinois and several other states, and confusion over how to interpret the results of the contest for electors in Alabama, cloud the issue of who really won the popular vote.[3] But, assuming that Kennedy had a 115,000 vote plurality, the shift of only some 13,000 votes (5,000 in Illinois, 5,000 in Missouri, 1,200 in New Mexico, 1,300 in Nevada, and 200 in Hawaii) would have made Nixon president. With the popular vote almost a "dead heat," it might be overstating the case to describe such an event as a "wrong winner" election, but it surely would have been considered unfair, provoked cries of "foul" from Kennedy supporters, and produced powerful demands for constitutional change.

The election of 1968 was another popular vote "dead heat," although the lopsided electoral college vote camouflaged that fact. Richard Nixon, once more the Republican standardbearer, received 31,785,480 popular votes to Hubert Humphrey's 31,275,166. The electoral college outcome was 301 for Nixon, 191 for Humphrey, and 46 for George Wallace. In spite of the extreme closeness of the popular vote, 1968 did not come as close to a "wrong winner" situation as one might have predicted. Nevertheless, it could have happened. Shifts of less than 1.5 percent of the voters in Illinois, Missouri, New Jersey, and Ohio (a total of about 154,000 votes) would have produced a Humphrey victory in the electoral college even though Nixon would still be left with a popular vote margin of over 200,000. A much smaller shift (1,095 voters in Alaska, 10,244 in Missouri, and 30,631 in New Jersey) would have denied Nixon an electoral college victory and thrown the election into the House of Representatives, a possibility discussed in detail in Chapter 3.

If 1968 could *theoretically* have produced a "wrong winner," the 1976 election contest between Carter and Ford *actually* almost did. It wasn't just theory. It very nearly happened. And it almost happened in an election in which the popular vote majority was clearcut.

What made a "wrong winner" a live possibility in 1976 was the closeness of the electoral college vote. The actual electoral vote count was Carter—297, Ford—240 (and one "faithless" Ford elector casting a maverick vote for Reagan). A shift of only 30 electoral votes would have elected Ford. (Actually, 29 would have done it, since the maverick Republican elector would almost certainly have stayed with Ford rather than having his vote elect a Democrat.)

A shift of only 9,300 votes (out of over 81 million cast), 5,600 in Ohio and 3,700 in Hawaii, would have elected Ford (by giving him Ohio's 25 electors and Hawaii's four), even though Ford would still have trailed Carter in the national popular vote by more than 1.6 million votes!

But earlier in the year another story altogether had played itself out in New York, with enormous consequence for a "wrong winner" scenario. The story focused on Eugene McCarthy, the former senator whose anti-Vietnam War election challenge to President Lyndon Johnson eight years earlier had scuttled Johnson's chances for re-nomination and reelection that year. In the summer of 1976, when it had become clear that a relatively conservative Southerner would win the Democratic nomination, McCarthy once more entered the presidential lists, announcing that he would launch an independent campaign. New York and California were to be McCarthy's particular targets, especially New York, where he had based his 1968 campaign and fund-raising efforts. McCarthy still had a following in New York; in the wake of his 1968 campaign his followers had established the New Democratic Coalition, a liberal reform bloc within the New York Democratic Party. This group had been prominent in the New York McGovern campaign in 1972 as well as in many local contests in the years since 1968.

The state's Democratic Party leadership was very concerned about the danger McCarthy could pose to the party's ticket in the New York presidential contest if his name was on the ballot. They believed that McCarthy could potentially attract enough liberal Democratic votes (perhaps between 100,000 and 250,000) to deny Carter a statewide plurality in a close contest and to deliver New York's 41 electors to Ford. The Democratic State Committee decided to challenge McCarthy's qualifying petitions in hopes of denying him a place on the state ballot. New York's election law is notoriously complex and stringent, designed to serve the interests of insiders and the party organizations. Moreover, the elected judges in the state who rule on such challenges owe their nominations and elections to the party organizations. In New York City that means the Democratic organization. And sure enough, the court ruled that the McCarthy qualifying petitions were deficient and ordered his name and elector candidates off the ballot. The state party knew what it was doing and history has vindicated its decision. As the election approached it became clear that New York was going to be very close. Had McCarthy's name stayed on the ballot and had he waged a vigorous campaign in New York, he might well have won five percent of the state vote. Had that occurred, Ford, rather than Carter, would have captured New York's electors and, with them, the presidential election, in spite of Carter's big lead (1.3 million votes) in the national popular vote.

Of course, when contests in particular states are as close as they were in 1976 in Hawaii, Illinois, Ohio, Pennsylvania, and New York, among others, other events, almost idiosyncratic in nature, can influence election outcomes. Another of those idiosyncratic events occurred in New York and might have altered the outcome and prevented a wrong winner in 1976. About a year before the election, at the height of New York City's financial crisis, President Ford had refused to support a congressional proposal for a federal government "bail-out" of the city in the form of guaranteed loans. The *New York Daily News*, the city's biggest circulation daily (and normally Republican in editorial outlook) reported the story with five-inch tabloid headlines reading:

FORD TO CITY:
"DROP DEAD!"

It is impossible to estimate accurately the impact of such an event, but it is not inconceivable that it could have cost Ford as many as a hundred thousand votes in New York City. Had Ford not alienated New York City residents with his highly publicized rejection of aid to the city, and if McCarthy had succeeded in getting his name on the New York State ballot, Ford would probably have won the election, thus becoming a "wrong winner" president.

Computer simulation of presidential elections has suggested that when the popular vote is as close as it was in the 1960 election, the odds of a "wrong winner" outcome are nearly 50–50. When the popular vote margin is as narrow as 500,000 votes, the odds of a "wrong winner" outcome are about one in three.[4] But, as we have just shown, a "wrong winner" can quite easily occur even in an election where the popular vote margin is substantial. In 1976, Ford could have won the electoral college vote while trailing Carter by over a million votes. And, contrary to conventional wisdom, we can even demonstrate that a wrong-winner outcome is quite possible in a presidential contest where the plurality is very large, in the 5 to 7 million vote range—an election like 1988!

"WRONG WINNER" POSSIBILITIES IN NOT-SO-CLOSE ELECTIONS

History records the 1988 contest as another "wipe-out" for the Democrats. The electoral vote was a lopsided 426 to 112. The popular vote was:

Bush   48,881, 278 (54 percent)
Dukakis 41,805,374 (46 percent)

Bush had a plurality of almost 7 million votes. And yet, in the final weeks of the campaign, the Dukakis strategists, having concluded from their polls that a popular vote victory was impossible, concentrated their efforts on achieving a "wrong winner" electoral college victory.[5] As late as election day, people in the Dukakis national headquarters felt that an electoral college upset was in the making. Bush's campaign staff was also concerned about the possibility. But how could such an upset happen in an election that wasn't even close? Isn't a "wrong winner" outcome possible only in tight contests? Let's see. Table 2.2 shows the state-by-state breakdown of popular and electoral votes in 1988.

Looking at the first part of the table, the states carried by the Republican ticket, focus on the right-hand column, labeled, "Wasted Votes." The lopsided victories Bush won in many of the states he carried meant that he "wasted" over 3 million votes. By contrast, Dukakis' narrower victories in the states he carried were much more "efficient" in electoral college terms.

If we focus on the vote percentages in the states that Bush carried, we can pick out the closely contested states where a small shift in the popular vote would have shifted the state from the Republican column to the Democratic. Table 2.3 outlines how eleven states emerge from such a review. If fewer than one percent of the nation's voters, concentrated in those eleven states, had shifted their votes from Bush to Dukakis, the Massachusetts governor would have won a "wrong winner" victory in the electoral college, 272 to 266, leaving Bush to console himself with his 5.8 million (!) vote plurality and the American people shocked and angry at the system's overriding of their clearly expressed preference.

Could Dukakis really have pulled off a "wrong winner" electoral college victory in 1988? The answer is "Yes, maybe." Some of his staff thought he could. In the last two-and-a-half weeks of the campaign, Dukakis had begun to hit back at the Republican smear tactics and to reclaim his party's liberal ideology. The polls were showing a recovery from the precipitous declines of August and September. Based on their daily polling and the trend lines that appeared, Dukakis strategists believed that they had a chance of eking out narrow victories in many of the states listed in Table 2.3 and, perhaps, pulling off an electoral college upset.

But it didn't happen. Bush did win. He carried the popular vote by a comfortable 54 to 46 margin and he won the electoral vote 426 to 111.[6] We didn't have a "wrong winner."

The skeptic might look at Table 2.3 and the Dukakis strategists' victory scenarios and say,

Table 2.2
Electoral Votes and Popular Votes—1988

EV*		Bush Vote** (%)	Dukakis Vote** (%)	Plurality**	"Wasted" Votes***
	Bush States				
9	Alabama	810 (60)	547 (40)	263	104
3	Alaska	102 (62)	62 (38)	40	17
7	Arizona	694 (61)	447 (39)	247	101
6	Arkansas	464 (57)	345 (43)	119	43
47	California	4,756 (52)	4,448 (48)	308	--
8	Colorado	728 (54)	621 (46)	107	27
8	Connecticut	747 (53)	675 (47)	72	8
3	Delaware	131 (57)	99 (43)	32	11
21	Florida	2,539 (61)	1,632 (39)	907	526
12	Georgia	1,070 (60)	716 (40)	354	141
4	Idaho	253 (63)	147 (37)	106	45
24	Illinois	2,299 (51)	2,181 (49)	118	--
12	Indiana	1,280 (60)	851 (40)	429	172
7	Kansas	553 (57)	422 (43)	131	46
9	Kentucky	731 (56)	579 (44)	152	50
10	Louisiana	881 (55)	716 (45)	165	51

4	Maine	304 (56)	241 (44)	63	21
10	Maryland	834 (51)	794 (49)	40	--
20	Michigan	1,969 (54)	1,673 (46)	296	75
7	Mississippi	552 (60)	361 (40)	191	77
11	Missouri	1,081 (52)	1,004 (48)	77	--
4	Montana	190 (53)	168 (47)	22	4
5	Nebraska	389 (60)	254 (40)	135	52
4	Nevada	206 (60)	133 (38)	73	30
4	New Hampshire	280 (63)	162 (37)	118	50
16	New Jersey	1,700 (57)	1,275 (43)	425	153
5	New Mexico	261 (52)	237 (48)	24	2
13	North Carolina	1,232 (58)	890 (42)	342	129
3	North Dakota	166 (57)	127 (43)	39	14
23	Ohio	2,412 (55)	1,935 (45)	477	152
8	Oklahoma	678 (58)	483 (42)	195	74
25	Pennsylvania	2,291 (51)	2,184 (49)	107	--
8	South Carolina	600 (62)	368 (38)	232	97
3	South Dakota	166 (53)	146 (47)	20	4
11	Tennessee	939 (58)	678 (42)	261	98
29	Texas	3,014 (56)	2,231 (44)	783	287
5	Utah	427 (67)	207 (33)	220	97
3	Vermont	123 (60)	116 (40)	7	1
12	Virginia	1,305 (60)	861 (40)	444	179
3	Wyoming	107 (61)	67 (39)	40	17

Table 2.2 (continued)

EV*		Bush Vote** (%)		Dukakis Vote** (%)		Plurality**	"Wasted" Votes***
	Dukakis States						
3	District of Columbia	26	(14)	153	(86)	127	60
4	Hawaii	159	(55)	192	(45)	33	10
8	Iowa	542	(55)	667	(45)	125	38
13	Massachusetts	1,184	(54)	1,387	(46)	203	50
10	Minnesota	958	(54)	1,107	(46)	149	33
36	New York	2,975	(52)	3,228	(48)	253	2
7	Oregon	58	(53)	575	(47)	67	7
4	Rhode Island	170	(56)	217	(44)	47	16
10	Washington	800	(51)	845	(49)	45	--
6	West Virginia	308	(52)	339	(48)	31	3
11	Wisconsin	1,044	(52)	1,122	(48)	78	--

* electoral votes

** in thousands

*** number of votes over 52% of the state's popular vote total, in thousands

Source: Harold W. Stanley and Richard G. Niemi, *Vital Statistics on American Politics* (2nd.) (Washington,

    D.C.: Congressional Quarterly, Inc., 1990), pp. 80–81.

Table 2.3
Vote Shifts Which Would Have Produced a "Wrong Winner" in 1988

Electors	State	Vote shift required to change outcome	% shift required to change outcome
47	California	154,000	1.6
8	Connecticut	36,000	2.5
24	Illinois	59,000	1.3
10	Maryland	20,000	1.2
20	Michigan	148,000	4.1
11	Missouri	39,000	1.8
4	Montana	11,000	3.0
5	New Mexico	12,000	2.4
25	Pennsylvania	54,000	1.2
3	South Dakota	10,000	3.2
3	Vermont	4,000	1.7
160		547,000 (0.6% of national vote)	

It's all very well for you to manipulate the voting numbers in such a way as to achieve a hypothetical wrong-winner result, but things don't really happen like that. Vote shifts of that sort, even if they occurred, are not likely to be so perfectly targeted. If any one of the changes listed in Table 2.3 or in the Dukakis scenario did not occur, then the whole wrong-winner script falls apart. It just isn't realistic.

That is a valid criticism. In the real world, things are not usually quite that tidy. Nevertheless, is it very easy to go down the list of states and, looking at their voting patterns in 1988 and in other recent years, to see future wrong-winner possibilities emerging, all with Democratic "beneficiaries." Remember that the underlying basis for any wrong-winner outcome is the large number of votes "wasted" by popular vote leaders in the states where they win by landslides. These wasted votes make them the popular vote leaders, while not adding to their electoral college totals.

In spite of recent historical precedent, it *is* still conceivable that a non-Southern Democrat *can* win the presidency. However, given the enormous popular vote advantage Republican presidential candidates have typically had in the last twenty years, barring some massive scandal, candidate health problem, or some other dramatic event, the odds of a Democratic popular victory would appear to be rather long. Let's look at the record. (See Table 2.4.)

Although recent history would indicate grim prospects for Democrats, a Democratic candidate doesn't need to win a popular plurality to win the presidency. Given the current political alignments in the states, it is quite possible that a strong Democratic ticket could, if it won 48 to 49 percent of the two-party vote, succeed in pulling off a "wrong winner" electoral college upset.[7]

Let us look again at at the 1988 returns and see how it might happen, starting with the states Dukakis actually won: New York, Massachusetts, Rhode Island, Iowa, Wisconsin, Minnesota, Washington, Oregon, West Virginia, Hawaii, and the District of Columbia. Three clusters of Democratic strength appear: the

Table 2.4
Distribution of the Two-Party Vote for President—1968–1988

Year	% Republican	% Democratic	Plurality
1968	50.4	49.6	.7
1972	61.8	38.2	23.6
1976	48.9	51.1	2.2
1980	55.3	44.7	10.6
1984	59.2	40.8	18.4
1988	53.9	46.1	7.8
20 Year Mean	54.9	45.1	10.6

Northeast, the upper Midwest, and the Northwest. Reviewing Table 2.2, we can see other states in these areas that were close enough to suggest that the Democrats could have a real chance of carrying them under other, somewhat better, circumstances. A future Democratic candidate could have charisma; Dukakis was dull. The campaign could be well managed; Dukakis' campaign made one error after another and remained on the defensive until the last two weeks before the election (he admitted later that he had run a "lousy" general election campaign.).[8] The economy might go into a slump, hurting the Republican's chances, unlike 1988 when the economy chugged along in a continuation of the longest expansion in post-war history.

If a couple of such reasonable contingencies actually occur, a Democratic ticket can not only carry the states Dukakis carried but also South Dakota, Missouri, Illinois, Michigan, and Ohio in the Midwest, Maryland, Pennsylvania, Connecticut, and Vermont in the East, and Montana, California, and New Mexico in the West. That would produce a clear electoral college majority.

One or two other states could also conceivably fall into the Democratic column, including Texas, New Jersey, Colorado, or Kentucky. Democratic popular vote margins in all of the non-1988 states would probably be quite narrow. Thus, while victories there would contribute to the Democratic electoral vote total, they would not add much to the Democrat's popular vote pluralities.

A future Republican candidate, meanwhile, can be expected to rack up the huge vote pluralities that have become the norm in the last twenty-odd years in the Old Confederacy, the western states of Utah, Idaho, Wyoming, Arizona, Nevada, Alaska, Kansas, Nebraska, Oklahoma, and North Dakota, and in other GOP strongholds like New Hampshire, Indiana, Maine, Tennessee, and Delaware. If the Republican ticket carried the twenty-six states just listed by the same pluralities that Bush did in 1988, and if the Democratic ticket carried most of the remaining states by fairly close margins, then a "wrong winner" outcome would be guaranteed. Bush's 1988 plurality in the states just listed exceeded 5.8 million votes, but only produced 181 electors. A Democratic candidate could expect landslide victories only in the District of Columbia and, perhaps, Rhode Island. The remaining states would be fought out by the two parties with the winner almost always in the 50 to 55 percent range, with narrow pluralities and with relatively few "wasted votes." And that is the anatomy of a "wrong winner" election in the 1990s. With the lopsided Republican majorities in the South, the interior West, and the other solidly Republican states, and highly competitive contests almost everywhere else, a future Democratic victor in a close presidential race is as likely as not to be a "wrong winner."

It has been quite popular among sophisticated journalists in recent years to refer to a "Republican lock" on the electoral college.[9] Even leading political scientists have embraced the notion that the Republicans have a "lock" on the electoral college.[10] One scholar has described the "lock theory" as follows:

> The lock theory simply took note that while Republican candidates for president had carried twenty-three states with

202 electoral votes in each of the five elections from 1968 to 1984, Democrats had consistently won only the District of Columbia, with its 3 electoral votes. Broadening the standard to include states that had gone for a party in four of the five elections only widened the disparity: 354 electoral votes (thirty-six states) for the Republicans, 13 electoral votes for the Democrats (D.C. and Minnesota). With 270 votes needed to win, the electoral college seemed to some to be so imbued with a Republican bias as to practically rig the election.[11]

As superficially appealing as it seems, the idea that Republican nominees have a lock on electoral college victory is extremely misleading. The use of the word "lock" implies that the Republicans gain some special advantage from the electoral college vote-counting arrangements that enhances their chance of winning. Nothing could be further from the truth. What the Republicans have had a lock on in the last two decades (and especially in the 1980s) is the *voters*. In the three elections in the 1980s, Democratic presidential candidates received a total of only 115 million popular votes while Republican candidates got 147 million! Republican candidates didn't win because of any special advantage the electoral college gave them. Quite the contrary. Far from providing the GOP with any built-in *advantage* in presidential elections, the electoral college actually makes the Republicans particularly *vulnerable* to a "wrong winner" electoral upset, in spite of their continued popular dominance at the polls. It is a *Republican* nominee, in this electoral era, winning those millions of "wasted votes" in the South and interior West, who is going to be denied the White House by an electoral college "wrong winner" misfire, not a Democrat. Far from guaranteeing Republican victory, the electoral college may succeed in snatching victory from the grasp of a Republican popular vote winner. Some Republican lock!

WHAT HAPPENS WHEN IT HAPPENS?

This whole book, including its title, is built around the premise that the electoral system is going to misfire in one of the next few presidential elections and produce an electoral college majority for a Democratic candidate who was defeated at the polls by a plurality of over a million votes. We have suggested that such a "wrong winner" outcome would have serious political consequences. Let us turn our attention to those consequences. What would actually happen if the electoral college made the wrong candidate president?

In one sense, nothing would actually happen. There would be no rioting or looting, no call to arms, no charges of "stealing the election." The United States is an extraordinarily stable political system with almost universal agreement on the rules of the game and enormous respect for the Constitution. Moreover, although the two parties are sometimes in rather sharp disagreement on important issues, both are seen as embracing mainstream system values, and both are seen as legitimate. Therefore, an inauguration committee would be formed, a Democratic transition team would be named, platforms and camera towers would be constructed on the West Portico of the Capitol, and the president-elect would be sworn in by the chief justice on January 20, just as always.

But, despite all of this evidence of stability and continuity, the election of a "wrong winner" would have serious political consequences. Probably the most serious of these would be the lack any semblance of mandate. There is, of course, nothing in the Constitution about presidential mandates. As drafted by the Framers, the selection of the president did not include provision for any direct participation by the people. In the early nineteenth century, however, virtually all of the states adopted popular election of presidential electors, who, by that time, had become mere partisan rubber-stamps for the state's majority voters.

Yet, in spite of the relative democratization of the presidential election process, there appears to be little sense that the presidency in the nineteenth and early twentieth centuries was the "people's office," that a president governed because of a "mandate from the people." In part, this can be explained by the nature of the party system and by the relative strength of Congress vis à vis the presidency in that era. Except in extraordinary times, especially wartime, the presidents from 1840 until the Great Depression did not play a very central role in the political system. Nominated by party bosses in the proverbial "smoke-filled rooms," these presidents from Harrison to Hoover were hardly a distinguished lot, and few of them, save Lincoln, Theodore Roosevelt, and Wilson, left their marks on American history or even on the politics of their own day. If there was a locus of peacetime power in that century, it was the Congress.

But revolutionary developments in the early twentieth century in economics, communications, and the international arena thrust the American president onto center stage and dramatically altered his constitutional role, making him, in the words of most introductory American government textbooks, "Chief Legislator," "Leader of the Free World," "Lobbiest for the People," "Party Leader," and "The Nation's Agenda-Maker." A well-known book on the presidency was even entitled *The Imperial Presidency*, conveying a sense of the enormous power and importance attached to the office.[12] And these powers and functions came to be justified and rationalized in terms of a "mandate from the people."

The significance of this change can be seen in the transformation of the presidential nominating process in the last four decades. In that short period of time, the power to choose the presidential candidates has been withdrawn from the leaders of the state political parties gathered in convention, and placed in the hands of the mass media and rank-and-file voters in the presidential primaries.[13] Nomination depends not on the support of various wings of the party leadership but on the support of voters in over thirty presidential primaries. The nominees carry a popular mandate direct from the voters.

In the general election campaign, a similar development has occurred. No longer are presidential campaigns run by the parties' national committee staffs but by separate candidate committees ("Citizens for Eisenhower," "The Committee to Re-elect the President," "Reagan-Bush Committee," etc.). A presidential victory has become a personal victory more than a party victory.

The ensuing government is the "Reagan Administration" rather than the "Republican Administration." The president's success in winning enactment of his legislative program has usually depended more on his "mandate" than it does on his party's strength in the national legislature. This was clearly illustrated by the congressional "batting averages" of Presidents Carter and Reagan. Carter defeated his opponent in 1976 by a narrow popular vote margin. Although there were Democratic majorities in both houses, he had great difficulty getting his legislative program through Congress. President Reagan, on the other hand, having defeated his incumbent opponent by a plurality of some 8 million votes, was hailed by the media and by the Congress as having a massive popular mandate. In spite of the fact that the Democrats had a majority in the House of Representatives, President Reagan succeeded in winning Congressional approval for virtually every part of his program in his first year in office. A triumph for mandate.

But, what happens to a president when the people's mandate has been given to the President-elect's *opponent*? To what extent can an administration rejected by the voters be effective in winning support in the Congress? Of course, we have had presidents in the recent past who had virtually no popular mandate. The near-tie votes at the polls in both 1960 and 1968 certainly placed some constraints on Kennedy and Nixon in their first years in office, although neither's administration could be said to be crippled by the lack of a clear popular majority. In both cases, however, the winner appeared to have a plurality of the popular votes cast and both had strong electoral college majorities to give them the *appearance* of a mandate.

A better example of a president without a popular mandate was Gerald Ford. Selected by Richard Nixon under the provisions of the Twenty-Fifth Amendment to replace the resigned Spiro Agnew, Ford had been neither nominated for vice president by national convention nor elected by the people. Ford had never been elected by any constituency beyond his home congressional district in Michigan. He took office, succeeding the disgraced

Richard Nixon, who had resigned the presidency rather than face certain impeachment by the House of Representatives. This is about as close as one can come to having no popular mandate, short of being a "wrong winner." (Of course, Andrew Johnson of North Carolina had found himself in 1865 with a really serious mandate problem when he was thrust into the White House by the assassination of Abraham Lincoln. He would pay for his lack of mandate with impeachment proceedings later in his term which came within one vote of removing him from office.)

To what extent was President Ford hampered by the lack of a mandate? For one thing, he had to cast numerous vetoes, illustrating his inability to win congressional support for his viewpoints and the absence of a popular mandate for his policies. In his twenty-eight months in office he cast sixty-six vetoes, twelve of which were overridden. By contrast, President Nixon, in his six-and-a-half years in office, had cast only forty-three vetoes, only five of which were overridden.

If Ford had serious political problems because he lacked any positive mandate from the electorate, how much more difficult would it be for a president to govern if the people had given their mandate to the *other candidate*? What would a president have to face if, after having been *rejected* by the people, he or she was inaugurated anyway?[14] Assuming that a contemporary wrong winner is likely to be a Democrat who would probably face a Democratic majority in at least one house of Congress and, perhaps, both, the problem might not be of crippling proportions. But what Democrat would want to attempt to govern in such a situation? The first Democratic president to be elected in almost twenty years, and winning on a fluke, on a technicality, in spite of having been rejected by the voters? What a pall that would cast over inauguration festivities! What a hollow ring "Hail to the Chief" would have as the Marine Band struck up the music! What a somber mood would prevail in the House chamber as the "People's (*Second*) Choice" delivered his or her first State of the Union address!

And what of our claim to be a democracy? Clearly the central legitimacy myth in the United States is that our leaders govern by virtue of their selection by the voters, under agreed-upon constitutional rules. In Gerald Ford's case, legitimacy rested on constitutional provision alone, there having been no election to fill the vacated vice presidential office. In a wrong-winner situation, constitutional provision again would provide whatever legitimacy there would be. Of course, that would be sufficient to assure orderly transfer of power and the new president a full term in office. However, a wrong-winner result would be accompanied by a countervailing, de-legitimating factor—the voters had chosen the *other* candidate. Unlike the Ford succession, an election *would* have been held and the president-elect would have *lost* the democratic contest, depriving him or her of the prime source of democratic legitimacy in modern-day America. Moreover, in a wrong-winner situation, the constitutional provision, the only source of legitimacy where there is no popular mandate, would *itself* be called into question.

One of the first orders of business of the new Congress after a wrong-winner election would be to begin hearings on proposals for a constitutional amendment to abolish the electoral college. Given the political realities and experience in the last twenty years, our lawmakers have so far decided to wait until the Constitution actually misfires before they take steps to correct the wrong-winner defect. The great disadvantage of this very "realistic" decision is that eventually the country will have to suffer four years of a seriously impaired wrong-winner presidency. Let us hope that the misfire occurs in a period when we can afford to tolerate a politically crippled chief executive. We might even hope that the nation has the good sense to eliminate the faulty electoral college machinery that makes such a misfire possible.

NOTES

1. For a thorough review of elections that have come close to a misfire over a 150-year period, see Neal R. Peirce and Lawrence D. Longley, *The*

People's President: The Electoral College in American History and the Direct Vote Alternative, rev. ed.(New Haven, Conn.: Yale University Press, 1981), chap 4.

2. Peirce and Longley, *The People's President*, p. 116.

3. William R. Keech, "Background Paper," in *Winner Take All: Report of the Twentieth Century Fund Task Force on Reform of the Presidential Election Process* (New York: Holmes and Meier Publishers, 1978), pp. 40–41.

4. Peirce and Longley, *The People's President*, p. 116.

5. E. J. Dionne, Jr., "Candidates Wage Battle to Dawn," *The New York Times*, November 8, 1988, p. A19; Paul Taylor and David Broder, "In the Closing Days, Dukakis is Betting on 18 States," *Washington Post National Weekly Edition*, October 24–30, 1988, pp. 12–13.

6. The total is one short of 538 because in the formal electoral vote, one Democratic elector voted for vice presidential candidate, Lloyd Bentsen, rather than for Dukakis, The "faithless elector" phenomenon is discussed in Chapter 6.

7. See Michael C. Nelson, "Partisan Bias in the Electoral College," *Journal of Politics* 36 (November 1974), pp. 1033–48. Nelson shows a pattern of Republican advantage in the electoral college in the 1930s, 1940s, and 1950s caused by all of the Democrats' wasted votes in the old "Solid South" shifting into a period of Democratic advantage in the 1960s as the voting realignment in the South and interior West creates big blocs of wasted votes for the Republicans. This advantage could create a Democratic "wrong winner" in close elections. In an article "Constitutional Aspects of the Elections," in Michael Nelson, ed., *The Elections of 1988* (Washington, D.C.: Congressional Quarterly, 1989), pp. 181–209, using the same methods, Nelson confirmed the Democratic electoral college advantage in 1988 (see p. 194).

8. "Dukakis Says Harm of Presidential Bid Was Unanticipated," *The New York Times*, January, 17, 1990, p. A17.

9. E. J. Dionne, Jr., "Analyzing the Electoral Vote: Does the G.O.P. Have a 'Lock'?" *New York Times*, October 12, 1988, p. A1.

10. Gerald M. Pomper et al., *The Election of 1988* (Chatham, N.J.: Chatham House Publishers, 1989), see frontispiece, pp. 74–75; James Q. Wilson, "Realignment at the Top; Dealignment at the Bottom," in Austin Ranney, ed., *The American Elections of 1984* (Durham, N.C.: Duke University Press, 1985), p. 308–9.

11. Michael C. Nelson, "Constitutional Aspects of the Elections," p. 193.

12. Arthur Schlesinger, Jr., *The Imperial Presidency* (Boston: Houghton-Mifflin, 1973).

13. Byron E. Shafer, *Bifurcated Politics: Evolution and Reform in the National Party Convention* (Cambridge, Mass.:, Harvard University Press, 1988), pp. 38–39.

14. See Theodore S. Arrington and Saul Brenner, "Should the Electoral College Be Replaced by the Direct Election of the President?" *P.S.* 17 (Spring 1984), p. 241.

3

Third-Party Mischief

If the electoral college method of selecting presidents isn't strange enough, with its potential for wrong-winner outcomes, it gets even weirder when third parties and independent candidates with substantial (or even meager) followings get into the act. There are two ways they can complicate elections terribly and wreak havoc on voters' choices under the ground rules of our system.

First, the Constitution requires the House of Representatives to select the president if no candidate gets a majority of electoral votes, which can happen *only* if there are more than two candidates or if there is an *exact* electoral college tie in a two-candidate race (a highly unlikely event). What this means is that where electoral votes are closely divided between the Democratic and Republican candidates, a third party can stymie an electoral college victory for either by winning a handful or less of states.

Second, the winner-take-all method of allocating electoral votes of each state that creates the potential for wrong winners (discussed in Chapter 2) and that results in so many group biases (to be discussed in Chapter 4) has still another undemocratic impact. It creates an exaggerated "spoiler" role by allowing third parties with modest numbers of popular votes to determine the allocation of large numbers of electoral votes. This can alter the outcomes in individual states by siphoning votes from the leading candidate, thus turning the putative loser into a winner who gets a big electoral vote bonanza.

Thus our presidential election system provides opportunities for third parties not only to boost their own power but to frustrate the will of the majority. As this chapter will show, these are not idle possibilities. Third parties have had substantial if not decisive impacts on elections past, and they have come perilously close on more than one occasion to turning the choice of the president into total disarray. Third parties, often dismissed by political scientists and others as rather insignificant in American politics, can in fact carry quite a wallop because of the electoral college system.

THROWING THE ELECTION INTO THE HOUSE

The Election of 1824

Selection of the president by the House of Representatives is not just a looming constitution specter; it has happened. The election of 1824 featured four serious candidates, all of whom had formidable credentials: John Quincy Adams (the secretary of state and son of John Adams, the second president); Henry Clay (speaker of the House of Representatives); William Crawford (secretary of the treasury); and Andrew Jackson (a general who was the hero of the Battle of New Orleans). In that year the electoral college had 261 votes, which meant that the winner had to get 131 votes to obtain a majority. But it turned out that the top vote-getter in the electoral college was Jackson with 99, 32 short of the "magic number" required for victory. Crawford and Clay received 41 and 37 votes, respectively, each getting *less than half* of Jackson's vote of 99 or runner-up Adams's vote of 84. The "also-rans" managed to block either front-runner from a majority, thus shifting selection of the president into the House of Representatives, which—interestingly enough—chose Adams, the number-two man in *both* the popular and the electoral college balloting![1]

The election of 1824 was really an *intra-party* contest as all four candidates were Democrats—the Federalist Party had faded out and had not yet been replaced by the Whigs or the Republicans. But although strictly speaking there was no "third party" (or even a second party!), Jackson and Adams were clearly the two major competitors, and the other two men were akin to third- and fourth-party candidates. The minor candidates, Clay and Crawford, could not win, but they were able to impede either major candidate from prevailing in the electoral college. The net result is a *classic* example of how contemporary third parties, although not serious contenders, could throw the election into the House of Representatives.

Close Calls

The election of 1824 is sometimes dismissed as a historic relic. Popular voting was minimal; in six states (including New York), electors were still chosen by state legislatures instead of by the voters; the notion of the "pledged elector" had not yet taken root; and the two-party system had not yet been established. To top this off, no "short list" of candidates had emerged to succeed two-term president James Monroe, whose "era of good feeling" had somewhat squelched the rise of national leaders. In a sense, the presidency was "up for grabs"—creating an almost unique opportunity for mischief-making at the hands of weak candidates.

But subsequent history has featured several close calls, elections where the House of Representatives alternative was avoided only by a hairbreadth. In fact, three out of the last eleven elections almost wound up in the House. In 1948, 1960, and 1968 relatively small shifts in the voting in *no more than two states* would have prevented either the Democratic or Republican candidates from obtaining a majority of electoral votes. These outcomes are summarized in Table 3.1.

In 1948, President Harry Truman won reelection with a scant 303 electoral votes, only 37 more than the required majority of 266; the Republican, Thomas Dewey, received 189; the remain-

Table 3.1
Recent "Close Call" Elections Almost Requiring the House of
Representatives to Choose the President

	Electoral Votes
_1948_	
Harry S. Truman (Dem.)	303
Thomas E. Dewey (Rep.)	189
Strom Thurmond (Dixiecrats)	39
Needed for election	266
Truman's "safety margin"*	37
_1960_	
John F. Kennedy (Dem.)	303
Richard M. Nixon (Rep.)	219
Harry Byrd (Ind.)	15
Needed for election	269
Kennedy's "safety margin"*	34
_1968_	
Richard M. Nixon (Rep.)	301
Hubert H. Humphrey (Dem.)	191
George C. Wallace (Amer. Independent)	46
Needed for election	270
Nixon's "safety margin"*	31

* A shift of this number of electoral votes away from the winner would have thrown
  the election into the House of Representatives.

ing 39 went to Strom Thurmond, who was the nominee of the
Dixiecrat Party, which had split off from the Democrats after they
adopted a pro-civil rights plank at their convention. Had Califor-

nia and Ohio gone for Dewey instead of Truman, which would have required a change of only 12,487 out of 3,365,925 votes cast in the two states, Truman's total electoral votes would have shrunk by 50 to 253—less than a majority. However, Dewey's gain of 50 would have netted him a total of only 239, leaving him also short of the victory threshold. This was a "close call" indeed: a shift of only *2/100 of one percent* of the national vote would have sent the election into the House of Representatives.

In 1948, Strom Thurmond's third party almost precipitated a crisis by carrying four states (Alabama, Louisiana, Mississippi, and South Carolina). In 1960 a group of unpledged electors (also opposed to civil rights) *from only two states* (Alabama and Mississippi) came close to preventing an electoral college majority for either Democrat John F. Kennedy or Republican Richard Nixon by casting fifteen votes for segregationist Harry Byrd of Virginia. A shift of only 8,971 votes in Illinois and Missouri would have switched those states from the Kennedy to the Nixon column, depriving Kennedy of the presidency by reducing his electoral vote count from 303 to the submajority number of 263 but leaving Nixon with only 259 electoral votes—also short of a majority.[2]

Thus, Kennedy really skated on thin ice. A minuscule vote shift of about 1/10 of one percent of the popular votes cast in two states would have enabled a fringe group of racial bigots to prevent the country from electing a president in its normal way. All kinds of chance events could have turned the outcomes around in these states: an impolitic comment by Kennedy during the campaign, antagonizing some small group or community and costing him a few thousand votes; an additional campaign appearance or two made by still-popular President Eisenhower on behalf of Nixon, which might have gained Nixon some extra votes; a flub made by Kennedy in the first nationally televised presidential campaign debates; a freak snowstorm keeping down the vote in a couple of Kennedy strongholds; and so forth and so on. The lesson? When the electoral college is rather evenly split between major candidates, splinter groups have enormous potential for enormously complicating the selection of a president and wielding power totally disproportionate to their support in the electorate.

Only eight years later, in 1968, the lesson was repeated: a nip-and-tuck election between the two major candidates was almost nullified by a third-party candidate who had no chance of winning the election himself but who was able to make it very difficult for either the Republican or the Democrat to amass a majority of electoral votes. The pattern was a familiar one, except that this time it was the Republican, Richard Nixon, who almost had *his* victory at the polls and *his* lead in the electoral college snatched away from him by a third-party candidate. Thus, Nixon got the same kind of political scare that his earlier opponent John Kennedy had received eight years earlier as a result of the strange rules for electing presidents.

This time the third-party mischief-maker was George Wallace, who as governor of Alabama was widely known for his part in resisting the integration of the University of Alabama. Wallace had much regional strength in the Deep South as well as modest support in parts of the North and West that were experiencing backlash against the civil rights movement. He won five states and received 46 electoral votes.

Even the numbers are strikingly similar to 1948 and 1960. Nixon's electoral vote total was 301, two less than the totals for Truman in 1948 and Kennedy in 1960, both of whom received 303 electoral votes. But with the passage of the constitutional amendment giving District of Columbia residents the right to vote, a minimum of 270 electoral votes was now necessary to win the presidency instead of the 266 needed by Truman and the 269 needed by Kennedy. Consequently, Nixon only had 31 electoral votes to spare.

The popular vote numbers game shows many paths to a disaster for Nixon and a decisive role for the House of Representatives. A one-state shift could have done it: if Nixon lost 111,674 votes in California, Humphrey would have won that state. The net result would have been 261 electoral votes for Nixon, 231 for Humphrey, and 46 for Wallace. If only 1.5 percent of the California electorate had changed its mind and voted for Humphrey, there would have been no electoral college winner.

If we consider multiple state shifts from one candidate to another, the possibilities of an electoral college stalemate are almost endless. If Humphrey picked up 67,485 votes more in Illinois and 30,632 votes more in New Jersey, his electoral vote total rises to 243 and Nixon's plummets to 258; Wallace's total remains 46. Again, no winner—with only a 1.5 percent switch in Illinois and a one percent switch in New Jersey.

Moving to three-state shifts opens up many possibilities, one of which entails movement of only 56,465 votes. If Humphrey had picked up 1,095 more votes in Alaska, 45,215 more in Ohio, and 10,245 more in Missouri, he wins those states. His electoral vote count jumps to 232; Nixon's drops under the majority cutoff point to 260; Wallace holds his 46. In this case, vote shifts by slightly *less* than one percent of the voters in these states produces a no-winner situation.

So far we have only considered changes in the Humphrey-Nixon popular vote allocations. If we put possible shifts in the Wallace vote into the hopper, all kinds of permutations become possible. If Wallace wins four additional Southern states where he in fact did very well (coming in *second* in three of them), he eats away at Nixon's slim majority and deprives him of the presidency. A 4.2 percent defection to Wallace in Tennessee, South Carolina, North Carolina, and Florida results in a surge of 45 in Wallace's electoral vote tally at the expense of Nixon, who falls to 256. Again, no winner emerges and the House of Representatives comes onto centerstage.

Finally, regarding 1968, consideration of scenarios where Nixon loses some states to Humphrey and others to Wallace opens the door to still more no-winner outcomes. One example will suffice to make the point. If Wallace gets 23,901 more votes in Tennessee and Humphrey obtains 10,245 more in Missouri and 30,632 more in New Jersey, Nixon's electoral vote majority also evaporates. Once more, relatively small amounts of vote-changing would have stalemated the electoral college and shunted the election to the House of Representatives.

These musings about 1968 are hardly fanciful. In the last few weeks of that campaign, Hubert Humphrey surged in the polls, having won back many defectors angry about his association as vice president with Lyndon Johnson's Vietnam War. Had the campaign lasted a few more days or had he received a little more support from other Democrats still resentful about the bitter struggle for the Democratic Party nomination, he might have won just enough extra votes to give him victories in the above mentioned states. Other "what ifs?" come to mind: If Lyndon Johnson had managed to get peace talks with North Vietnam underway, Humphrey would clearly have benefited at the polls. Had the crookedness of Nixon's running-mate Spiro Agnew come to light in 1968 rather than five years later when he was forced to resign the vice presidency, surely Nixon would have lost a sizable batch of votes to Humphrey. Because the margins of victory in so many states were so small and the implications in terms of potential electoral vote shifts were so great, the alternative outcomes sketched above were well within the realm of plausibility. In 1968, we were clearly on the brink of a House of Representatives selection of the president.

So there you have it: six elections between 1948 and 1968, three of which came within a whisker of producing electoral vote breakdowns that would have failed to elect a president. All it takes is a relatively close contest between the two major parties in the electoral college and a third party or independent candidacy capable of winning a few states. The analysis of Chapter 2 should be borne in mind: Due to the wasted vote phenomenon, closeness in the electoral college can occur despite a fairly large popular vote plurality for the winner. If the loser ekes out victories in a number of big states and the third party squeaks to victory in a few states, together they can command sufficient electoral votes to out-poll the popular vote winner in the electoral college. Popular vote losers may get insufficient electoral votes to become "wrong winners," but when joining forces with third parties they

can derail the "right winner" and force the election into the House
of Representatives. Our little journey back to three recent elections shows us that this is not some wild fantasy dreamed up by
political scientists but a perfectly realistic possibility.

What makes these speculations even more unsettling is the
powerful bargaining potential of third parties or independent
electors. Remember, electors are not constitutionally bound to
the candidates they support; they are perfectly free to vote as they
choose. Had Truman failed to achieve an electoral vote majority,
Thurmond's electors in 1948 could have put their votes up "for
sale," voting for Truman in exchange for his willingness to resist
civil rights advances. Had Kennedy received between 251 and
265 electoral votes in 1960 (instead of the 303 he actually got),
the 15 unpledged electors who voted for Harry Byrd in 1960
would have held the pivotal votes to put Kennedy over the top and
might well have attempted to extract such an anti-civil rights
commitment from him as the price of getting their support.
Indeed, there is evidence that between November 8 (election day)
and December 19 (when the electors met to vote) Byrd delegates
unsuccessfully tried to swell their numbers by getting Kennedy
electors from the Deep South to defect to Byrd and give him just
such leverage by reducing Kennedy's electoral total to below the
magic number of 266.[3]

Had George Wallace won a few more states or Nixon lost a
few more, Wallace would have been in a similar position in 1968.
Nixon won less than three percent of the Black votes[4] and had
already apparently made a deal with Senator Strom Thurmond of
South Carolina to "go easy" regarding civil rights in exchange
for Thurmond's support (yes, this is the same Thurmond who
came close to being the "kingmaker" in 1948!). So Nixon would
have been under intense pressure to bargain with Wallace, perhaps
exchanging his promise to withdraw federal voting registrars in
the South or to refrain from initiating any more suits challenging
segregation in return for Wallace's electoral votes. All kinds of
agreements are possible if a major party candidate is just short
of electoral college victory and the minor candidate engages in

"hard ball" politics.[5] Unscrupulous? Perhaps. Constitutional? Absolutely!

Do not regard these scenarios as fantasies. Wallace himself, fully recognizing that he was incapable of winning a majority of electoral votes, early in the campaign candidly embraced the goal of becoming a power broker in the electoral college. He said that it was his intention, if neither Nixon nor Humphrey got the 270 electoral votes requisite for election, to go to each and ask: "What will you give me if I make you president?"[6] It was his plan to instruct electors committed to him in states that he won to abandon Wallace himself and instead vote for the candidate with whom Wallace had worked out a deal.

As the popular vote race became closer and an electoral college deadlock began to loom as a realistic possibility, some electors began thinking about counterstrategies to preempt a role for Wallace. One such plotter was novelist James Michener, a Humphrey elector from Pennsylvania. He decided that if Nixon won the popular vote but failed to get an electoral vote majority, he would urge the Democratic and Republican leadership to work out a compromise under which Nixon would win the presidency but grant concessions to the Democrats such as the inclusion of some of their number in the Cabinet. He and some other electors were prepared to defect from Humphrey and vote for Nixon rather than permit Wallace to yield power. Said Michener: "Stated bluntly, if Wallace intended to play the game he said he was playing, I intended to beat him to the punch."[7]

All of this became moot when Nixon eked out an electoral college victory. But there is precedent for such dubious politicking when the presidency is up in the air. In 1876, the election between Republican Rutherford Hayes and Democrat Sam Tilden was rampant with corruption. Outcomes in several states were challenged. Although Tilden won the popular vote (as was discussed in Chapter 2), Hayes was in a position to win by one vote in the electoral college if three of the disputed states went his way. Congress ultimately created a commission composed of five senators, five House members, and five Justices of the

Supreme Court to resolve matters. Ostensibly their mission was to sort out the conflicting vote returns and determine who were the true winners in the states of Louisiana, Florida, and South Carolina. But in fact they worked out one American history's most infamous political deals having nothing to do with what happened at the ballot box: Hayes would get all three contested states and the presidency in return for agreeing to end Reconstruction in the South, essentially endorsing the concept of White supremacy. This sordid agreement relegated Blacks to second-class citizenship and poisoned race relations for a century, but almost anything is possible when the presidency is in the offing. If a few out-of-the-mainstream electors hold the balance of power in the electoral college (as they almost did in 1948, 1960, and 1968), 1876-style bartering could well become the order of the day.

What, then, does the future portend? Are the cliff-hangers of the past harbingers of political nightmares to come? The answers to these questions depend on two factors: (1) whether there are electoral college landslides, in which case third parties have little power, and (2) whether any third-party candidates on the horizon have the potential for carrying one or more states and their electoral votes. As for the first, although the Republicans triumphed mightily in the 1980s, all kinds of unpredictable factors could enable the Democrats to become competitive in the years to come. Recessions, unpopular wars, and scandals are but a few of the contingencies that could resurrect the Democrats, not to mention the emergence of an especially attractive candidate. The Democratic Party is now weak when it comes to presidential elections, but it is hardly dead.

The second factor, third-party strength, is more uncertain. The elections of 1948, 1960, and 1968 all featured candidates with formidable regional followings. Indeed, all three were candidacies based on appeals to White supremacy and resistance to racial integration. But now that millions of Blacks are voting in the South and many Whites in the South have softened their anti-Black attitudes, it is questionable whether a resurgence of third parties appealing to White racism could carry any states. It is worthy of note in this regard that George Wallace became quite pro-Black in his final terms as governor of Alabama, and that a Black man, L. Douglas Wilder, was elected governor of Virginia in 1989. And, although there is some evidence of a resurgence of anti-Black sentiment—such as the political success of former Ku Klux Klan leader David Duke in Louisiana—it now seems improbable that White candidates inveighing against Blacks can establish an electoral college beachhead enabling them to throw a presidential election into the House.

On the other hand, there are other possible independent candidacies appealing to frustrated or embittered groups in the population that could emerge as viable challengers to the established parties. The most obvious source of a third party is Blacks feeling let down by both the Democrats and the Republicans. Jesse Jackson won nearly all the votes of Blacks in the Democratic Party primaries of 1988, and there is little doubt that he could command the allegiance of many Blacks if he ran as an independent in a general election.

The crucial question is whether he could win any states. Undoubtedly he could carry the District of Columbia, which is 71 percent Black, but it is unlikely that he could carry any states since no state has a majority of Blacks and the state with the largest proportion of Blacks (Mississippi) is only 35 percent Black. Even if he did carry one or two states, his campaign, appealing largely to Black voters who are one of the core Democratic Party constituencies, would all but doom the Democrat's prospects in the rest of the country, leading to a Republican electoral college landslide victory. Thus, a Black third-party insurgency would not be likely to force an election into the House of Representatives.

Are there any other incipient threats to electoral college majorities lurking in the background of American politics? Probably not, but there are a few states so dominated by certain groups that they could well become arenas for third parties to mobilize voters. Hispanics, the fastest-growing group in the

American population, could conceivably cluster around the Spanish-speaking candidate appealing to their interests and win some southwestern states. And although even less likely, a radical ideologue on the left or the right of the political spectrum could carry the day in one or two states, as happened in 1924 when Progressive candidate Robert La Follette won Wisconsin's 13 electoral votes. Most Americans have eschewed third parties, but social conditions that produce extreme anger or frustration in certain demographic groups could well cause alienated groups to reject mainstream parties. Should this happen sometime in the future, electoral college majorities will again be imperiled, and the unpredictable House of Representatives contingency election procedures will again be pressed into service.

HOUSE OF REPRESENTATIVES' CHAOS

The Constitution says precious little about the ground rules for House of Representatives' choice of the president. Article II simply states that the House must choose one of the three top vote-getters in the electoral college, that each state gets one vote, and that a majority vote is required to win. That's it.

What is left unclear is just how each state congressional delegation is to cast its single vote. This is obvious in states that have only one congressperson (such as Alaska and Rhode Island); that person alone decides how the state will go. But what happens in multiperson delegations? Presumably, each state caucuses, and whichever candidate comes out ahead receives the vote of that state.

This general understanding leaves many questions unresolved. Is it the "new" House, elected the same day as the presidential election, that votes, rather than the "old," which is ready to leave office? Apparently the new. What happens to a state's vote if there is a tie within a state? The Constitution is silent on this matter. And since there are three presidential candidates involved, what would happen within a state delegation if no one candidate had a majority? The answer is totally unclear.

But these ambiguities in the technical rules pale in comparison with the uncertainty about the proper criteria to be used by House members. Since we have only had one election in the House of Representatives, and *that* over a century-and-a-half ago, no customs or norms have evolved to guide the House. In 1824, each House member enjoyed the freedom to reach an independent choice, which resulted in intrigue and machinations having nothing to do with the general election. But that was before the era of the pledged elector and long before the democratization of American politics that created the presumption that the people should pick the president. It also was prior to the rise of media politics, which has focused public attention on congresspersons' votes and made them vulnerable to retaliation at the polls if they seriously antagonize their constituents. So if an election should again devolve onto the House, the past provides no guidelines whatsoever; all bets are off.

Should the House be called upon to select the president, there are actually four alternative philosophies that could determine each member's vote. These are the options available:

1. A member could decide that democratic ideology required him or her simply to ratify the outcome of the *national* popular vote;

2. A member could see himself or herself as a mere rubber-stamp of the decision that the *state's* voters made at the polls;

3. A member could act strictly as a partisan politician voting for his or her own party's candidate regardless of how that candidate had fared in the representative's own state or in the nation;

4. A member could act autonomously and simply vote for the presidential candidate of his or her own choice.

The results of a House election would vary dramatically depending on which course members chose. This is illustrated in

Table 3.2, which simulates House elections in the three years discussed earlier when such an outcome was narrowly avoided. In this examination, we look at what would have happened if California and Ohio had gone Republican in 1948, if Illinois and Missouri had gone Republican in 1960, and if California had gone Democratic in 1968. It will be recalled that in all three of these contingencies no candidate would have received the electoral vote majority; the elections would have moved to the House.

In 1948, Truman would win if the House simply rubber-stamped his popular vote victory; he would also win if all members of Congress followed their state voting returns—since Truman, even without carrying California and Ohio, would have taken twenty-six states (one more than the minimum of the twenty-five necessary for a majority). However, if all the votes were cast along party lines, a totally muddled picture emerges: Democrats would control twenty-one delegations, Republicans twenty, Dixiecrats four, with three delegations evenly split between Democrats and Republicans (presumably losing their votes).[8]

Just as opportunities for vote trading loom in the electoral college when no one gets a majority, so too does the specter of such political shenanigans appear where neither candidate receives a majority of states. Thus, the Dixiecrats who apparently had the sympathy of members of Congress in four states would be in an ideal position to deliver the presidency to Truman—of course demanding some quid pro quo. A small party that won only 2.4 percent of the popular vote might have been able to force its terms on a president.

In 1960, had Illinois and Missouri wound up in Nixon's column instead of Kennedy's, results in the House would also have been indeterminate. In that election there were widespread allegations of fraud in Illinois, among other places, and it is questionable whether many Republicans would have seen fit simply to ratify Kennedy's popular vote victory. Had all members of Congress reflected statewide returns, Nixon would have prevailed because he would have won twenty-eight states. But the result would have

Table 3.2
Winners in Simulated House of Representatives Elections

	1948	1960	1968
	California and Ohio vote for Dewey	Illinois and Missouri vote for Nixon	California votes for Humphrey
1. Winner if all House members ratify popular vote	Truman	Kennedy	Nixon
2. Winner if all House members follow state popular vote	Truman	Nixon	Nixon
3. Winner if all House members vote along party lines	Unclear	Unclear	Humphrey
4. Winner if all House members make independent judgment	?	?	?

been completely unpredictable had party loyalty guided House members because the new party line-up after the 1960 elections would have been twenty-three states controlled by regular Democrats, six controlled by Deep South Democrats not at all happy with the prospect of a Kennedy presidency, and seventeen controlled by Republicans; four delegations were evenly split. Again, what would happen if allegiance to party guided votes is anyone's guess.

The same confusion would have prevailed in 1968 had California gone for Humphrey. The popular vote was so evenly divided (31,785,148 for Nixon to 31,274,503 for Humphrey) that House members might have felt less constrained about rubber-stamping the popular vote outcome, especially since Nixon's total vote was only 43 percent of the total—well below a majority. Had state popular vote results guided the representatives, Nixon would have retained his victory because, even without California, he would have won thirty-one states. On the other hand, voting the "party line" would have jeopardized Nixon because it was the Democrats who controlled twenty-six congressional delegations. And if that does not muddy the waters enough, it must be realized that a few of the Southern delegations might well have bolted from Humphrey, since Nixon's political views were closer to the sentiments of the White constituents who still dominated their districts. All in all, the situation would have encouraged bargaining of the most nefarious kind: Democrats could have elected Humphrey (the popular vote loser!), but he might have had to make peace with Southern Democrats to secure their votes and in the process turn his back on the Blacks who were the backbone of his electoral support. What political turmoil would have been created because the electoral college failed to produce a winner!

Perplexing as this analysis of House of Representatives voting may seem, it is even more confounding than it appears. First of all, individual House members probably would have conceptualized their roles quite differently: *Some* would just ratify the choice of the voters nationally; *some* would act in a representative capacity and echo the outcomes in their states; *some* would stick with their political party no matter how the voters had acted; and *some* would act autonomously. The net result would be an utterly chaotic voting pattern.

Second, if outcomes looked very close, congressional blocs might concoct strategies that would enable them to wield influence. A bloc of Blacks or women might see this as an opportune time to exercise bloc power by extracting concessions from candidates and voting accordingly. So even if party voting became the general order of the day, some might break ranks, and those in evenly divided states might break ties on the basis of promises made to their groups. Closeness within state caucuses and within the House as a whole provides great temptation for interests that have theretofore felt powerless to flex their muscles.

Finally, an even more insidious form of seduction might take place. Presidential candidates could entice members of Congress with "sweeteners"—promises of *personal* benefits to be had if they voted the right way. Possibilities abound: promises of presidential appointments for themselves or their protégés; assistance in future campaigns; support for legislation helpful to a member's state or district; access to the White House after the election. Such "side-payments" are hardly new in American politics; presidents in office routinely use them to win over wavering legislators whose votes they need to pass key legislation. Surely, politicians might deign to use the same tactics when the stakes were even greater—the presidency itself.

There is still another threat to democratic principles inherent in contingency elections in the House. Even if House members refrain from some of the unseemly practices discussed above, the *weighting* of the votes to be cast is totally out of line with any conception of "one person, one vote." The bias in favor of small states explained in Chapter 4 is compounded if the House elects the president, because each state would have the same vote power regardless of population. The smallest state, Alaska, with its 546,000 people gets *one* vote; the largest state, California, with its 29,000,000 people gets *one* vote; those in between such as Oklahoma with its 3,000,000 people get *one* vote. Or to make the same point another way: the 25 largest states in which 85 percent of the people live have the same representation as the 25 smallest states where 15 percent of the people live. Of course, this kind of malapportionment is perfectly constitutional since it is the Constitution itself that clearly mandates one vote per state when the House elects the president. But that does not make it right.

Thus, the House of Representatives' alternative is a mess—unwieldy, unpredictable, and unfair. It permits the voters' choice to be undone; it sets the stage for unsavory politicking; it gives undue power to small blocs of House members; it gives minor candidates undeserved leverage in choosing the president; and its gives small states excessive power. The ability of third parties to thrust this horror on the nation is, in itself, a serious indictment of the electoral college system.

Failure of either major party to get an electoral college majority would create one additional problem, sinking the nation even deeper into a political quagmire. The Constitution specifies that the *Senate* picks the vice president if the electoral college fails to give either vice presidential candidate a majority. Failure of any presidential candidate to get a majority would almost certainly subject vice presidential candidates to the same fate because electors almost always vote for both candidates on the same ticket.

The Senate, however, would be free to follow its own course in selecting the vice president apart from what the House does. Because its makeup often is quite different from that of the House, and because its members have different constituencies (whole states instead of relatively small districts), the Senate decision could be at odds with that of the House. Indeed, there have been any number of instances where one party had a majority in the Senate while the other had a majority in the House (as in 1981–1982), so it is by no means far-fetched to imagine the two bodies of Congress picking a president and a vice president of opposite parties. We could well have a repeat of 1796: two archrivals leading the country in the same administration. *This* is political madness—one that third parties could inflict on the nation because of the strange rules of the electoral college.

Crazy as this scenario sounds, there is an even more bizarre possibility: election of *no* president at all. Several things could happen to prevent any candidate from getting a majority of votes in the House, which is the constitutional requirement for election. The state delegations could be evenly divided, twenty-five for one candidate and twenty-five for the other. A number of states might be evenly split internally, that is, two members for the Democrat and two for the Republican; this would preclude the state from voting, making it all the harder for either candidate to muster up twenty-six votes needed for election. The third-party candidate might also win one or more states, another contingency that would make it difficult for the major candidates to win an adequate number of states.

What would happen next is anyone's guess. Perhaps the Senate would have elected a vice president, in which case he or she would become "acting" president until the House deadlock was resolved. But what if the Senate too were to get bogged down, as might happen if the third-party candidate got some votes and neither major party candidate could secure the necessary fifty-one votes? Presumably the Speaker of the House would become president under the terms of the Presidential Succession Act, which puts the Speaker next in line for the presidency. What a fiasco that would be: Someone who did not even run for national office and who was elected by about half a million people from a small geographic area would become president of the United States. This may seem like the plot of a contrived political novel, except for one thing: it could happen. If no one wins in the electoral college owing to an even slightly successful third-party candidacy, political chaos might well be in the offing.

THIRD PARTIES AS SPOILERS

Third parties pose another problem. By taking some votes away from the leading candidate, they can cause the less-preferred second-choice of the voters to come out ahead. Therein lies the origin of the word "spoiler": they cannot win on their own, but they can spoil it for the leader. When there is a relatively close race between the two major candidates, a third-party candidate can siphon away enough votes from one to allow the other to win. And since they often share more in common with the party they help defeat than the one that benefits, they can effectively thwart majority will.

This role is possible under various election methods, including direct popular election. There have been occasional three-party races for a United States Senate position that have resulted in just such a frustration of the majority. The 1980 Senate race in New

York, the returns from which are shown in Table 3.3, is a case in point.

To understand New York politics, one must know that in addition to the Democrats and the Republicans there are two other parties in that state—the Conservative and the Liberal. Normally, they support one of the candidates of the two major parties, but sometimes they run their own candidate. In 1980, Senator Jacob Javits, a liberal Republican, was successfully challenged in the Republican primary by Alfonse D'Amato, a quite conservative Republican. But rather than fade quietly into the sunset after several terms in the Senate, Javits mounted a last-ditch effort to stay in office by garnering the nomination of the Liberal Party. The Democrats ran Elizabeth Holtzman, a liberal Brooklyn congresswoman well known for her role in the Nixon impeachment hearings, whose views in many respects were similar to those of Javits.

What happened? Plainly put, Javits spoiled the election for Holtzman. Despite the fact that he was a sure-loser, his die-hard supporters gave him 664,544 votes. In the eyes of most observers, 75 to 85 percent of Javits's support would, in fact, have gone to Holtzman in a two-person race. The net result was that the Democratic and the Liberal candidates split the left-of-center vote, allowing Republican D'Amato to win with only 45 percent of the popular vote.

As long as election rules make it feasible for third parties to get on the ballot, these somewhat perverse outcomes will occasionally happen. Displeasure with major party choices can cause defection within the dominant party, and with it the opportunity for spoiling that party's chances in the election. However, the electoral college system amplifies this prospect by enabling small inroads into a major party's support to result in enormous electoral votes losses. It is the state-by-state winner-take-all component of the system that is again responsible: In a close election it takes only a small fraction of the total popular vote to tilt a state's entire allocation of electoral votes from one candidate to the other. A third-party effort in only one or two contested

Table 3.3
The 1980 New York Senatorial Election Results

	Popular Vote	Percent
Alfonse D'Amato (Rep. & Cons.)	2,699,652	44.9%
Elizabeth Holtzman (Dem.)	2,618,661	43.5%
Jacob Javits (Lib.)	664,544	11.0%
Other	32,057	0.5%
TOTAL VOTE	6,014,914	99.9%

states might very well "spoil" the presidential outcome for the whole nation.

The fascinating election of 1948 again looms large. Much is made of the role played by third-party candidate Strom Thurmond, whose Dixiecrats came close to preventing a Truman victory by winning sufficient electoral votes to almost deprive Truman of his majority. What is often forgotten is the more subtle role played by a fourth-party candidate, Progressive Henry A. Wallace, who received almost the same number of popular votes as Thurmond but failed to carry any states. The views of Thurmond and Wallace were almost diametrically opposed, but, ironically, it was Henry Wallace's candidacy that propelled Thurmond to his nearly decisive role. Truman was slightly to the left on the American political spectrum, and Wallace was considerably to the left of Truman; consequently, almost *all* of Wallace's votes were siphoned away from Truman. This cost Truman four states (Connecticut, Maryland, Michigan, and New York) where Wallace's vote count exceeded Dewey's plurality over Truman. This was no small potatoes; the four states accounted for 82 electoral votes. Without Wallace on the ballot, Truman's electoral total would have been a hefty 385—impervious to Thurmond's foray. Candidate Wallace, who got only 2.4 percent of the popular vote nationally, almost snuffed out Truman's election because his modest success in winning *popular* votes exacted a heavy toll from Truman in *electoral* votes. This is the spoiler's gambit *par excellence*.

It is not the *size* of the third party's following that is decisive but its *location* that determines its power in the electoral college system. In 1980, Representative John Anderson received a substantial number of votes from people dissatisfied with the choice between Republican Ronald Reagan, who at the time seemed too conservative, and President Jimmy Carter, who was thought by many to be a bumbler. Winning nearly seven percent of the popular vote was no mean feat for a relatively obscure congressman, virtually unknown outside his home state of Illinois a year before the election. Yet his impact on that election was meager not only because his support came from both disaffected Democrats and Republicans but because there were very few competitive states; Reagan had most of the states "sewed up." Because Anderson drew his votes from both major parties, and because his vote affected virtually no state outcomes, he had little impact on the presidential election.

On the other hand, a candidate who managed to get only 756,691 out of 81,555,889 cast nationally almost cost Jimmy Carter the presidency the first time Carter ran. The troublemaker was Eugene McCarthy, who eight years earlier had quite successfully challenged President Lyndon Johnson in the Democratic Party primaries with his anti-Vietnam War candidacy (although Hubert Humphrey ultimately got the nomination). In 1976, when Carter was running against President Gerald Ford, McCarthy ran again. This time he ran as an independent, articulated a rather amorphous set of positions on all kinds of issues, and went nowhere.

However, he did get enough votes from those caught up in 1968 nostalgia or disgusted with the "Establishment" candidates to make some noise in a few states—and those few votes almost cost Jimmy Carter the presidency! His biggest thunder was in California, where he received about 225,000 votes, substantially more than Ford's margin of victory of 139,960. Losing California and its whopping 45 electoral votes brought Carter's national electoral vote total down to 297, only 27 above the minimum necessary to get a majority. Other states that seemingly went to Ford because of McCarthy's presence on the ballot were Iowa, Maine, and Oregon, representing another eighteen votes. Moreover (as described in Chapter 2), had McCarthy managed to get on the ballot in New York, Carter might well have lost New York to Ford and, with it, the election. This conjecture aside, what would otherwise have been a relatively comfortable Carter victory was not decided until sunrise the morning after the election and came very close to producing a "wrong winner" outcome. In our system, small splashes of third parties or independent candidates can produce very wide ripples.

The potential for future spoilers abounds. Although the elections of 1984 and 1988 witnessed negligible third-party input in the presidential elections, this is probably a temporary disappearance. There is disquietude in the nation in many quarters, and it is under such circumstances that third parties germinate.

There is a "big time" spoiler waiting in the wings. Blacks have routinely furnished a huge chunk of the Democratic Party's voter coalition, going back to Franklin D. Roosevelt's election in 1932. A high point was reached in 1976 when their strong support for Jimmy Carter was a key to his success. But they have generally been lukewarm about their place in the coalition and they have often felt let down by the results. Thus, although Carter as president did appoint far more Blacks to judgeships and other high federal government positions, he hardly made civil rights and poverty concerns cornerstones of his presidency. No one likes to be taken for granted, least of all voters with pressing needs that have largely gone unmet in the national politics of recent years.

Recent elections are a case in point. Mondale received 89 percent of the Black vote in 1984 (to Reagan's nine percent) and Dukakis got 86 percent (to Bush's 12 percent).[9] But both Mondale and Dukakis to a greater or lesser extent tried to camouflage their liberalism (the much-dreaded "L-word") and seemed far more concerned with appealing to White voters than to Blacks. Black turnout at the polls was rather low, perhaps an indication of a voting group ready to break off from the Democratic Party and throw its support elsewhere, should an attractive opportunity present itself.

This is not mere speculation. We have Rev. Jesse Jackson's incredible success in the Democratic Party's primaries of 1988 as evidence of Black eagerness to vote for someone who is not only of their own race but clearly devoted first and foremost to their cause. Jackson was the second largest vote-getter in an original field of eight Democratic candidates, and he received nearly 7 million votes, the lion's share of which came from Blacks. Not only that, but he mobilized droves of new voters to register and stirred others who had not voted in years. No candidate vying for the presidency has mobilized Blacks the way Jackson did.

After receiving some assurances that the Democrats would pay attention to Black interests during the campaign, and after having his "day in the sun" as a prime-time orator during the Democratic National Convention in Atlanta, Jackson agreed to stay in the Democratic Party fold and even did some campaigning for Dukakis. But a couple of crucial questions come to mind: What would have happened in 1988, and what might happen in years to come, if Jackson or some other popular Black candidate forms a separate party specifically oriented to Black concerns, one that fields its own candidate in the general elections? Would such an independent political movement doom Democratic efforts to recapture the presidency?

The answers are straightforward. A serious third-party effort by Blacks would absolutely devastate Democratic Party chances. This can be demonstrated by supposing that someone like Jackson had run in 1976 when Democrat Carter won. Such a candidate would have pulled many Black votes away from Carter. We can simulate this situation by subtracting Jackson's 6,800,440 primary votes in the thirty-eight states where he ran in 1988 from Carter's totals in those same states. The result is striking: Carter would lose 15 out of the 24 states he carried, leaving him with an electoral vote of 74 to Gerald Ford's 464! Even if only half of these voters defected, Carter's state victories would diminish from 24 to 17 and he would only get 145 electoral votes—still resulting in a comfortable Ford margin in the electoral college. And if only 20 percent of Blacks jumped from the Democratic ship to support a third-party candidate of their own race, we would get a "wrong winner": Carter would keep a nationwide plurality of over 300,000 votes but he would lose the election as his electoral vote would drop to 249 (to Ford's 289). Many states were close in that election, so it would have been easy indeed for a viable Black candidate to spoil Carter's triumph.

Any Democratic presidential candidate would suffer a similar fate. Were Jackson to have run as an independent in 1988 and had all his primary supporters stuck by him, Dukakis' electoral vote would have fallen from 112 to 41! Dukakis' loss in the electoral college was so substantial that further losses that might have developed may seem insignificant. But had Dukakis been able to narrow the gap between himself and Bush a bit more than he did in the final two weeks of the campaign, the costliness of an independent Black candidate in the fray would be more apparent. There is simply no way that a Democrat can win if large numbers of Blacks abandon the Democratic ship.

An important caveat is in order. Blacks could function in similar fashion under a system of direct election; their desertion might well deprive a Democrat of his or her popular vote margin of victory. In a close or even a not-so-close election, this blow to the Democrats would be tantamount to handing the presidency to the Republicans, who would lose almost nothing from an independent Black candidacy because so few Blacks vote Republican anyway. A third party with enormous support that steals votes from one candidate only is always a spoiling threat, whether or not there is an electoral college.

However, it is the little imps on the political scene more than the dragons whose role as spoilers gets magnified by the electoral college. It is the single-issue groups feeling anger toward mainstream politicians who might decide to field an independent candidate capable of getting a million votes or so. One can well imagine the right-to-life movement trying to have some impact at the polls should current efforts to restrict abortions fail. Nor is it hard to conceive of the freedom-of-choicers using the ballot to protest should abortions rights get turned back; for some people it is about the only issue worth fighting for. And there are other issues that might at some point generate sufficient passion to provide grist for a third-party candidacy; examples include the right to own guns, religious fundamentalism, and homosexuality. In a close election, it is splinter groups dealing with matters such as these who can use the winner-take-all feature of our system to their advantage by costing candidates clumps of electoral votes despite limited appeal at the polls. Just as Eugene McCarthy almost cost Jimmy Carter the presidency, it is the tiny third party that is able to exercise disproportionate influence on presidential election outcomes that bears watching in upcoming years. Our electoral procedures give them quite an opportunity for power—if they choose to use it.

Normally, special interests do *not* run candidates for president. Rather, they use the implicit threat to bolt from the major parties to get leverage within them—a practice that one political scientist likens to "blackmail."[10] Democrats *must* listen to Blacks; Republicans *must* pay heed to anti-abortionists.

Both parties offend their constituent groups at their own peril, running the risk of having them boycott the polls (at best) or establish a third party (at worst). The exaggerated influence of such groups stemming from their inordinate capability of swinging electoral votes if they do run an independent candidacy can enable them to exact concessions from the parties with which they are generally aligned. Spoilers can get power by staying out of the election as well as by getting in.

NOTES

1. For a detailed account of the 1824 election of the president by the House of Representatives, see Neal Peirce, *The People's President: The Electoral College in American History and the Direct Vote Alternative* (New York: Simon and Schuster, 1968), pp. 82–86.

2. In fact, Kennedy's margin of victory was even smaller than Truman's even though they both received 303 electoral votes because the granting of statehood to Alaska and Hawaii had expanded the electoral college to 537 and raised the majority necessary to elect a president to 269.

3. Peirce, *The People's President*, p. 106.

4. "Portrait of the Electorate," *The New York Times*, November 10, 1988, p. B6.

5. In the 1960s some White supremacists in the South embraced the "free elector" plan whereby electors would be unpledged to any candidate and would instead bargain with the major party candidates to get anti-civil rights concessions. However, political scientist Gerald Pomper argued that the plan was doomed to failure because bargains would be hard to consummate in light of the constitutional prohibition against federal officials serving as electors and the control that national politicians would have to keep dissident electors from defying the voters' choice. What Pomper overlooked is that in a very close election, only a handful of electoral votes would be necessary to tilt the election from one candidate to the other. A few power-hungry or fanatical electors might well be willing to put their votes up "for sale" and thus control the election of the president. For Pomper's argument, see his "The Southern 'Free Elector' Plan," *Southwestern Social Science Quarterly* 45 (June 1964), p. 16–25.

6. Quoted in James Michener, *Presidential Lottery: The Reckless Gamble in Our Electoral System* (New York: Random House, 1969), p. 14.

7. Ibid., p. 21.

8. Although the Constitution says nothing about this, the precedents of 1800 and 1824, when the House of Representatives elected the president, imply that states forfeit their vote if there is a tie in the delegation.

9. "Portrait of the Electorate."

10. Theodore S. Arrington and Saul Brenner, "Should the Electoral College Be Replaced by Direct Election of the Presidency? A Debate," *P.S.* 17 (Spring 1984), p. 241.

4

Electoral College Biases

In the last two chapters we described the electoral college's potential for producing wrong winners, triggering a chaotic House of Representatives election of the president or encouraging third-party mischief. As if that were not enough, the electoral college system also contains a set of inherent biases that make the votes of some groups of citizens count much more than the votes of others in presidential elections.

STATE BIASES

Small-State Bias

The first set of biases appears to give undue weight to the votes of citizens in the smaller states. The apportionment formula in the Constitution assigns electoral votes to the states as follows: "Each State shall appoint . . . a Number of Electors equal to the whole Number of Senators and Representatives to which the State may be entitled in the Congress." Thus, by virtue of the fact that each state is entitled to at least two senators and one representative, even the smallest state receives three electoral votes. This automatic assignment of three votes to each state results in giving "bonus votes" to the smaller states, since the three electors they are automatically given are more than they "deserve" on the basis

of their population share. For instance, Alaska, the least populated state, had according to the Census of 1980, a population of
402,000, or *2/10 of one percent* of the nation's population. On
the basis of population share, Alaska "deserved" only one elector
(actually *.95* of one elector). In the actual case, Alaskans select
three electors, a "bonus" of two electoral votes. Table 4.1
compares the actual *1980s* electoral vote allocation for the ten
smallest states to the electoral vote they "deserved" on the basis
of their share of the nation's population alone. As the right-hand
column indicates, each of the smallest states gets a "bonus" of
one or two electors as a result of the constitutional apportionment
formula.

Table 4.2 illustrates the maldistribution at the other end of the
spectrum, showing the electoral vote "penalty" suffered by the
largest states because of the three-vote minimum provided for in
the Constitution.

As the two tables demonstrate, the constitutional apportionment of the electoral college in the 1980s gave the ten smallest
states a "bonus" of 14 electors while it "penalized" the ten largest
states 35 electors they "deserved" on the basis of their population
shares. Overall, twenty-five states and the District of Columbia
receive "bonus electors,"[1] seventeen got penalized one or more
electoral votes,[2] and only eight got their "fair" share.[3]

Large-State Bias

The inherent bias in favor of the small states is modest in terms
of numbers of electors, misallocating only 42 electors out of a
total of 538. This modest small-state apportionment bias is *more
than offset* by a much larger countervailing bias favoring the
largest states, one that results from the winner-take-all feature of
the electoral college system and from the patterns of two-party
competition in the states. Because all of the states (except Maine)
have an automatic winner-take-all system of choosing electors,
in a close popular vote contest the thousand or so voters who cast
the deciding votes in one of the smaller states would affect the

Table 4.1
Actual Electoral Vote versus "Deserved" Share of Electoral Vote: Ten Smallest States—1980s

	Number of Electoral Votes	Share of Electoral Votes	Share of 1980 Population	"Deserved" Electoral College Votes	Number of "Bonus" Votes
Alaska	3	.6%	.2%	1	2
Wyoming	3	.6	.2	1	2
Vermont	3	.6	.2	1	2
Delaware	3	.6	.3	1	2
District of Columbia	3	.6	.3	1	1
North Dakota	3	.6	.3	2	1
South Dakota	3	.6	.3	2	1
Montana	4	.7	.3	2	2
Nevada	4	.7	.4	2	2
New Hampshire	4	.7	.4	2	2

partisan distribution of only the three or four electors assigned to their particular state. By contrast, the marginal thousand voters in a very close race in New York in the 1980s would have decided the distribution of 36 electors and a similar number of California voters would have determined the fate of 47 electoral votes! Thus, a few thousand voters in the two largest states could control the choice of almost a third of the electors needed to select a president! This means that the "vote power" of voters in a large state is much greater than the "vote power" of those who live in a small state.

A good part of this countervailing large-state bias is simply a mathematical reality. In computerized studies, using elaborate mathematical models, researchers have found that the relative vote power (the chance that any voter has of affecting the election of the president through the medium of his or her state's electoral votes) of voters in California and New York is more than two times that of voters in some other states.[4] These

Table 4.2
Actual Electoral Vote versus "Deserved" Share of Electoral Vote: Ten Largest States—1980s

	Number of Electoral Votes	Share of Electoral Votes	Share of 1980 Population	"Deserved" Electoral College Votes	Electoral College Vote "Penalty"
California	47	8.7%	10.4%	56	9
New York	36	6.7	7.8	42	6
Texas	29	5.4	6.3	34	5
Pennsylvania	25	4.6	5.2	28	3
Illinois	24	4.5	5.0	27	3
Ohio	23	4.3	4.8	26	3
Florida	21	3.9	4.3	23	2
Michigan	20	3.7	4.1	22	2
New Jersey	16	3.0	3.3	17	1
North Carolina	13	2.4	2.6	14	1

studies reveal the interaction of the countervailing big-state and small-state biases. The two or three smallest states have relatively high vote power (1.6 to 1.8 times that of citizens in the most deprived state) because of their apportionment advantage. The great majority of the states have relatively low vote power, (about 1.3 times that of the most deprived state) because of their modest number of electors. But the ten largest states have quite high vote power, with the five largest of them having *very* high vote power, indeed (roughly 2 to 2.5 times that of the most deprived state). Although this kind of mathematical analysis is complicated (one noted scholar described it as "elaborate elucidation of the obvious by methods which are obscure"[5]), it clearly illustrates the enormous influence of a handful of voters in the largest states whose votes may determine the election of 25 to 50 electors.

This mathematical big-state vote power advantage is further exaggerated by the fact that vigorous two-party competition is typical in most of the large states but is not nearly so common among the small states. That means not only that the largest states have big and potentially crucial electoral vote totals but also that because of the close two-party competition that characterizes them, these big blocs of electors are potentially winnable *by either party's candidate* in a competitive national contest. States like California, New York, Pennsylvania, Ohio, Michigan, Illinois, Texas, and Florida, with their enormous blocs of electors, are potentially winnable by presidential candidates of either party. In a close national contest, they are often carried by narrow margins and are, therefore, ardently courted by candidates of both major parties.

By contrast, most of the states with fewer than ten electoral votes are presidentially noncompetitive. Most of the southern states and most of the smaller western and mountain states have been overwhelmingly Republican in recent presidential elections. Some other small states like Rhode Island, the District of Columbia, and Hawaii are heavily Democratic. Only about a quarter of the small states can be described as normally competitive, that is, close, decided by narrow vote margins.

Given the numbers of electors at stake in the larger states and the predictable closeness of their popular votes, presidential candidates and their strategists typically place tremendous emphasis on six or seven of the largest states and four or five of the more competitive middle-sized states like Maryland, Wisconsin, Washington, Missouri, and New Jersey. Meanwhile, a noncompetitive state, especially one with few electors, is typically written off by the candidate who is disadvantaged there and taken for granted (and largely ignored) by the candidate with the heavy advantage in the state, as both camps try to allocate rationally their scarce resources of time and money.

Let us look at Utah, for example, with its five electors in 1988. Utah's average Republican vote in the four previous presidential elections had been 68 percent. Even a strong Democratic candidate would stand little chance of winning this Republican bastion (Utah had not gone Democratic in a presidential election in over a quarter-century). The Dukakis campaign wisely decided to write the state off. But so did Bush's strategists, in a way! Knowing that their candidate would probably carry the state by almost a two-to-one margin, Republican campaign planners knew that they did not have to include Utah in their list of priority concerns. If Utah was to be courted by the Bush campaign at all, it would be in the context of general Republican appeals to the western and mountain Republican constituencies as a whole. The same could not be said of Texas or California, which, because of their size (electoral votes) and the realistic hope in both camps that they were winnable, became crucial battlegrounds where both parties' candidates fought for every single vote. As a result, individual voters in California and Texas had more political importance than individual voters in Utah, Idaho, Alaska, Rhode Island, and other small states with few electors and lopsided party preferences. In contrast, in a direct vote system, without the state-by-state winner-take-all feature, a voter in Salt Lake City would have as much importance as a voter in Houston or San Diego.

Bias Against Rapidly Growing States

Another inherent bias in the electoral college system grows out of basing state electoral vote allocations on population figures established by the decennial census. For states with rapidly growing populations this means that, as the decade progresses, their electoral vote allocation, because it is frozen for ten years until the results of the next census are known, becomes less and less equitable.[6] This is illustrated most dramatically by California. On the basis of the Census of 1980, California was allocated 47 electors. But the Census Bureau estimated that, by 1988, the population of California had reached 29 million, which would have entitled it to 54 electoral votes, instead of the 47 votes it actually cast. Other high-growth states like Florida and Arizona are similarly penalized. On the opposite end of the spectrum, the states with relative declines in their share of the nation's population benefit by this apportionment lag, both in electoral college influence and in congressional representation and power.

Bias Against States With High Voter Turnout

In addition to the vote power biases affecting the states because of their size, the electoral college system also has a strong bias against voter turnout in many of the states. This turnout bias results from the winner-take-all feature of the electoral college and the "wasted vote" phenomenon that we referred to in Chapter 2. Under the current system, the only voters' votes that really "count" are those that are cast for the candidate who wins the state. Those who vote for the losing candidate(s) "waste" their votes. But so do many of those who vote *for* the state winner! The only votes a winning candidate really needs are those necessary to guarantee that candidate an unchallengeable margin over the opposition. Any votes received over that number are "wasted," that is, unnecessary in order to win the state's electors. Those voters could just as well have stayed home.

The consequences are somewhat different for those who voted for the state winner and the voters who supported the losing candidate in the state. Those who voted for the state loser effectively had their franchise taken away—they lost their vote for president, since the state's *whole* electoral vote went for the *other* party's candidate. In fact, not only did they lose their votes—they had them *taken away* and assigned to the *other* party's candidate, since the state winner was given 100 percent of the state's electors, although that candidate might only have received 51 percent of the state's vote.[7] Under such a system, there is almost no incentive for the Democrats to rally potential Democratic voters in the traditionally lopsidedly Republican strongholds of Idaho, Utah, Nebraska, Arizona, Alaska, Indiana, North Dakota, or New Hampshire, or for the Republicans to turn out their voters in the District of Columbia. It doesn't make sense to devote a lot of energy, manpower, and money to produce votes that won't "count." Thus, the electoral college system removes a major systemic incentive for minority party-building in the one-party presidential states.

If, on the other hand, there were a direct vote system, the Democratic Party's success in turning out a thousand more Democrats in Republican strongholds like Salt Lake City or Boise would be crucial as its efforts to get a thousand more voters out in Democratic bastions like Philadelphia or Detroit, since every extra vote turned out would count and would count equally. The same would be true of Republican efforts in overwhelmingly Democratic Washington, D.C., Providence, or Boston.

But, ironically, in one-party dominant states, there is also little incentive for the *majority party* to maximize its voter turnout, either, because of the "wasted vote" phenomenon. In a state where the dominant presidential party is likely to get over 60 percent of the vote in any case, what incentive is there to push for even more votes? They aren't needed.[8] Many of the dominant party's votes are already likely to be "wasted" anyway, since the only votes that really count are those needed to provide a clear margin over the other party's candidate. Any votes over 51 or 52 percent don't matter anyway, so why bother to push for maximum turnout in a state you've already won?

The upshot is that voter turnout is not very important to *either* party in many of the states because of their noncompetitive nature. Put another way, presidential campaigns can largely ignore voters in the states where there is one clearly dominant presidential party. That is the very situation that exists in almost half the states! On the other hand, voter turnout is crucial and candidates of both parties *do* concentrate their time, resources, and issue attention on states where their efforts might spell the difference between carrying the state and losing it. The larger the electoral vote a close state has, the more attention it will get. And, given the distribution of presidential party competition in the current period, the states that will get the greatest attention are the competitive giants—California, New York, Illinois, Michigan, Ohio, Texas, Pennsylvania, and Florida.

In the discussion above, we pointed out the fact that in the noncompetitive states, neither the dominant presidential party nor the weaker party in a state has much incentive to maximize voter turnout. Since none of the players have much to gain by marginal increases in turnout, overall voter turnout in the noncompetitive states is lower than it might be if both parties in those states were pushing for their maximum number of votes, thus contributing considerably to the United States' extraordinarily low voter turnout rate.

But, there is a second bias against voter turnout in the electoral college system, quite different from the first. The apportionment of electoral votes to the states, after the standard allotment of three electors to each state, is based on the census of population. States with equal populations will have equal numbers of electoral votes. That certainly seems fair and proper. However, different states have different *turnout* rates. For example, Minnesota and Louisiana are almost identical in population. Both had ten electoral votes after the 1980 census. But, in the 1988 presidential election, the number of voters who went to the polls in Minnesota was 29 percent higher than the number who voted in Louisiana. So, although almost 500,000 more Minnesotans than Louisianians voted, both states cast 10 electoral votes. That worked out to about 210,000 Minnesota voters per elector and 163,000 Louisiana voters per elector. Other examples of benefited low-turnout states included Mississippi, with 133,000 votes per elector, Arkansas, with 138,000, and South Carolina, with 123,000. Thus, the electoral college always gives relatively greater weight to the votes of citizens in low-turnout states and less weight to those in high-turnout states, in a sense, punishing states for their high levels of citizenship. What an irony!

ADVANTAGED GROUPS

Not only is the electoral college biased in favor of some *states*, it also favors some *groups* over others. It bestows extraordinary political power on particular groups of voters while it capriciously denies a fair share of voting power to other groups of equal or greater size. The benefited groups are located in the large competitive two-party states in which their votes for one party's candidate or the other's hold the key to the election of the state's bloc of electors and, perhaps, even the national election's outcome.

Jews

Jews provide the clearest example, although there are other groups that are similarly benefited. While only about three percent of the national adult population is Jewish, the great majority of the Jewish population lives in the key electoral states of New York, Pennsylvania, New Jersey, Illinois, Michigan, Ohio, Florida, and California. Many of these states, especially California, New York, Illinois, Michigan, and Pennsylvania, are very competitive in close presidential contests, with the popular vote margin often much smaller than the total Jewish vote. Not only is the Jewish electorate strategically located, it is also highly participant, with very high voter turnout. But, beyond that, the Jewish vote, although traditionally heavily Democratic, has proven to be "movable" on issues relating to Jewish life, especially policy toward Israel.[9] Given the traditional closeness of the party balance in the key states, and the realities of recent presidential voting patterns, it is absolutely imperative for the Democrats to maximize their Jewish votes if they are to have much hope of carrying those key states and winning the presidential election. Since winning the Jewish vote is virtually mandatory for the success of the Democratic ticket, *splitting* the Jewish vote is one of the surest ways of ensuring victory for the *Republicans*. If the Republican candidate can win 25 to 35 percent of the Jewish vote in three or four of the key electoral states, especially New York and California, that vote could well provide the Republican margin of victory in those states in a tight race, denying the Democrats any possibility of an electoral college majority.

As a result of these electoral college realities, both parties' platforms and both sets of candidates vie against each other in a contest to prove that they are the firmest supporters of Israel and the most trustworthy guarantors of its security. So powerful is the electoral logic for both parties that serious foreign policy alternatives, such as support for the establishment of a Palestinian state, may be closed to the United States by virtue of the Middle East policy commitments made by the presidential candidates of both parties as they seek the support of the strategically crucial Jewish voters.

Italians

Another group geographically positioned to have maximum leverage in the electoral college system is the Italians. Like Jews, Italians tend to be concentrated in big electoral states like New York, New Jersey, Pennsylvania, Illinois, Ohio, California, and Massachusetts, many of which are closely competitive. However, although Italians outnumber the Jews somewhat, they are not as unified as a political force, do not have as distinct a political agenda, and have a lower voter turnout rate, so they do not have as much political impact as the Jewish vote. Nevertheless, given the historic division of their party loyalties between the Democrats and the Republicans, and their strategic location in the big industrial states, Italians are a very tempting target for both parties in the battle for electors, giving them political weight in presidential contests out of proportion to their actual numbers.

The Republicans have long recognized the strategic importance and great potential of the Italian vote. Although traditionally part of the urban Democratic coalition (except in parts of New England), Italians have shown more and more willingness to register and vote as Republicans. Italians are now the largest single ethnic group in the tri-state suburban region around New York City that, especially in New York state, holds the electoral balance between the traditionally Democratic urban vote and the traditionally Republican rural vote.

The trick for both parties has been to get a "hook" on the Italian vote. Lacking any clear-cut nationality issue equivalent to the Israel issue for Jews, the Democrats have approached the Italians with traditional Democratic economic appeals and with Italian candidates like Mario Cuomo and Geraldine Ferraro, the Democratic vice presidential nominee in 1984. As is common with many ethnic groups, Italians are very receptive to candidates of their own ethnicity. Republicans have gone after the Italian vote with appeals to patriotism, strong national defense, and family values, anti-abortion stands, law-and-order rhetoric, and veiled appeals to racial prejudice. Moreover, as Italian-Americans have moved up the socioeconomic ladder, Republican conservatism has become more appealing to them.

Suburbanites

It is not only ethnic groups that can have their political influence magnified by the electoral college voting system. Another sector of the electorate whose influence is greatly exaggerated by the electoral college system of counting votes is the residents of the suburbs in the big industrial states.[10] In many of these closely contested big electoral vote states, the political geography tends to be tripartite, with the central cities being overwhelmingly Democratic and the rural and small town counties being heavily Republican. The partisan political balance is often held by the suburban areas, where old-line Protestant Republicans have been joined in the last thirty-five years by urban expatriates, many of whom are Democrats. These newly arrived Democrats, most of whom have retained their traditional Democratic Party loyalties, have "evened up" the suburban party balance. As a result, the suburban and exurban rings around the central cities have become the focus of statewide races and of the presidential contests as well. The candidate who carries the suburbs carries the state. Given the pivotal position of the suburban voters in a closely contested, winner-take-all race, and given the enormous importance of these states in the electoral college, it is easy to see why the presidential candidates spend so much time and attention on big-state suburban voters and their concerns.

Narrowly Defined Economic Interests

Particular economic groups can also find themselves empowered by the luck of their geographic location. A good example of an economic group that benefits from electoral college geography is dairy farmers. Their clout is based on their highly organized and movable bloc vote and their strategic location in crucial two-party states like New York, Pennsylvania, Ohio, Illinois, Michigan, and Wisconsin, among others. Hopes of winning the dairy farm vote in the crucial swing states has motivated both presidential parties to bid for the dairy vote with price support promises that are costly to consumers and that, if there were no electoral college, would probably not be an important part of presidential candidate concern.

Labor unions are another example of particular economic groups whose power and political leverage is potentially magnified by the electoral college. Since unions have been most successful in organizing workers in the industrial states, union members tend to be concentrated in the big, competitive electoral states where their votes are assiduously courted by the candidates of both parties. Democratic candidates have to maintain the loyalty of the unions and their members if they are to carry the big industrial states they must have to win the presidency. Republican candidates try to peel enough union voters away from the Democrats to deny them those crucial states. In the process, unions and their memberships get more attention than their numbers alone might otherwise warrant.

DISADVANTAGED GROUPS

Just as some groups are advantaged by the electoral college, others are disadvantaged. There are some ethnic, social, and economic groups whose memberships are as large as the Jews or

Italians or the dairy farmers who are not equally benefited by the electoral college. In fact, some of these groups actually have their vote power and, therefore, their political clout significantly *diminished* by the system.

Northern Blacks

One group that comes immediately to mind is northern Blacks. Blacks living outside the South are concentrated in the key electoral states, especially in their metropolitan centers, where they make up a significant proportion of the states' electorates. In many of the key states, the Black vote is considerably larger than the Jewish or Italian votes.

However, unlike those groups, the Black vote has been almost monolithically Democratic in recent presidential elections. Given the rock-solid unanimity of the Black electorate, the Republican Party has not found it profitable or desirable to court the growing middle-class Black vote in the key states, choosing, instead, to go after other marginal vote groups, like Italians and other White ethnics, suburbanites, and blue-collar workers, for whom implicit racist appeals, like the infamous "Willie Horton" Republican commercials of 1988, may be quite effective.[11]

Any serious Republican attempt to appeal to middle-class Black voters would necessitate a shift away from such tactics and might be counterproductive for Republican efforts to consolidate their position with the White marginal vote groups they have been courting. Moreover, since Republicans have no guarantee that their appeals for Black votes would be effective in the actual event, simple prudence militates against such a shift in tactics, whatever its moral appeal.

Thus, northern Blacks, although they have gained considerable influence within the *Democratic* Party by virtue of their essential contribution to that party's electoral fortunes, have *failed* to win the leverage they would be able to have if *both* parties vied for their support as the parties do for Jewish votes. Therefore, in spite of their highly advantageous geographical distribution, which scholars have often argued gave them great and compensatory political influence on the presidency (especially noted in the Truman-Kennedy-Johnson era) to compensate for their numerical weakness in Congress, northern Blacks actually have only a fraction of their potential electoral college clout because of their inability to get the *two* parties to compete for their votes. This situation is likely to continue until a significant number of Black voters show themselves willing to cast their ballots for a Republican presidential candidate.

Hispanics

Hispanics also have potentially great electoral leverage because of their geographical distribution. However, the political role of Hispanics is complicated by two factors:

1. The political differentiations between Puerto Ricans, Cubans, and Mexican-Americans, and

2. The fact that many of the Hispanics are not citizens, and are ineligible to vote.

Let us look at a number of Hispanic groups, starting with the Cuban-Americans who are geographically concentrated in south Florida. At the time of their arrival in Miami, the Cubans lacked American citizenship. However, over the years, more and more Cuban-Americans have become naturalized. In the 1980s the American-born children of the earlier Cuban immigrants began to come of age. Together, naturalized and native-born Cuban-Americans now make up a significant proportion of the Florida electorate. The leadership of the Cuban community is anti-Castro, conservative, business-oriented, and pro-Republican. The Cuban vote has been a significant factor in every Republican presidential victory in Florida in recent years. The anti-Castro foreign policy of both national parties in attributable in part to the politics of winning Florida's electoral votes, as the Republicans reward their

Cuban supporters and the Democrats seek to peel Cuban votes away to their side. This bipartisan catering to the anti-Castro Cuban vote in the electorally pivotal state of Florida may limit American policy alternatives in much the same way as appeals to the Jewish vote restrict American policy options in the Middle East.

Puerto Rican-Americans make up the second significant group of Hispanic voters. Concentrated in New York, New Jersey, and the other northeastern states, Puerto Ricans, like Blacks, are disproportionately poor, urban, and Democratic. And, like northern Blacks, although they live in highly competitive two-party states with big electoral college votes, they are more or less taken for granted by the Democrats and written off by the Republicans.

Unlike Cubans or Mexicans, Puerto Ricans are already American citizens and thus eligible to register if they live on the mainland. However, Puerto Rican voter turnout is lower than almost any group, robbing it of influence. On top of that, the low socioeconomic status of most Puerto Ricans tilts them naturally toward the Democrats and makes Republican appeals for their votes unlikely. Thus, failing to win attention from the Republicans and failing to turn out strongly for the Democrats, Puerto Ricans have been denied the presidential clout their population numbers and strategic geographical location might seem to promise them.

By far the largest and most politically significant group of Hispanics is the Mexican-Americans, the *chicanos*. Decades of migration of Mexicans into the southwestern states has recently turned into a flood, as hundreds of thousands of Mexicans flee the poverty and lack of economic opportunity south of the border and migrate to the United States. California, Texas, and the less populous southwestern states already have relatively large Mexican-American citizen populations. As more *chicanos* become naturalized and as more U.S.-born Mexican-Americans attain voting age, and as Mexican-American populations spread to other parts of the country, their vote power can be expected to increase dramatically, if *both* parties compete for their support. If, on the other hand, ethnic political polarization occurs in the states where the *chicanos* are concentrated and the Democratic Party in those states comes to be seen exclusively as the party of the poor and the Blacks and the Mexicans, with the Republican Party representing the White middle-class majority, those states could move into a semi-permanent Republican mode, denying the Hispanic vote any meaningful presidential role, whatever.

Southern Blacks

Such a fate has already befallen *Southern* Blacks. Unlike their northern counterparts, Southern Blacks find themselves typically casting votes for president that have virtually no influence on the electoral votes of their states. The cause of their electoral impotence is the fact that Southern Blacks vote for the party in their states that is the perennial presidential loser there. Since the passage of the Voting Rights Act in 1965, when Blacks won their clear right to vote in the region, only one Democratic presidential candidate (Jimmy Carter of Georgia) has won *any* electoral votes in the South. Carter carried almost all of the Southern states in 1976, when he ran as the first major-party Southern standardbearer in over a century. In 1980, Carter won only his home state of Georgia, as the White voters in the region returned to their heavily Republican presidential voting pattern.

In each of the Southern states, in every one of those presidential elections, Black Southerners voted overwhelmingly for the Democratic candidate. With the stunning exception of 1976, when Southern Black votes were the undisputed key to Gov. Carter's electoral college victory (and Georgia in 1980), Black Southerners' presidential votes have been meaningless and without any political impact whatever. Democratic presidential candidates have generally soft-pedaled their appeals to Southern Blacks as they have typically returned again and again to that "dry well" represented by conservative White Southern Democratic voters. Republican candidates, making their appeal to "New South" White conservatives and alienated "good old boys" have made no attempt to win Black presidential votes. The result is that Southern Blacks have had little more influence on most modern presidential general elections than Bulgarians. Their votes, although technically cast, have usually not counted.

Homosexuals

Another group strategically located in the key electoral states, with high voter turnout, a high degree of political consciousness, and a definite political agenda does not have the kind of leverage the electoral college might be expected to give it. Homosexuals, a significant political group in a number of key states, find themselves in presidential politics in a situation remarkably like that of northern Blacks. Homosexuals, as a group, find the more liberal Democratic Party much more responsive to their concerns and far more open to their full-fledged participation in the presidential selection process than the Republicans. The more conservative Republican Party, whose political orientation is hostile to homosexuality, neither seeks nor receives the support of homosexual groups. It is probable that any attempt by the Republican leadership to court the homosexual vote, even if it chose to do that, would create internal disagreement and backlash among other potential Republican voting groups. Thus, like northern Blacks, urban homosexuals, because of their existing pro-Democratic loyalties and because of their negative image among more conservative groups, fail to get the political leverage on the presidency to which their location, size, organization, and turnout might otherwise entitle them in the electoral college system if both parties competed for their pivotal votes in the pivotal states.

Mormons

Another group denied its fair share of political importance in the electoral college system is the Mormons. There are nearly as many Mormons in the United States as Jews.[12] However, instead of being located in key electoral states, they are either widely scattered across the country or heavily concentrated in the sparsely populated and heavily Republican states of Utah and Idaho, states that have very few electoral votes and that, as we have seen, are either written off or taken completely for granted by the two major party presidential candidates. Mormons are also so heavily Republican that the Democrats don't see much percentage in going after their votes, especially since there are hardly any electoral votes there to gain. The Mormons are almost as far out of it in presidential elections as Southern Blacks are, although they do command five to nine electoral votes.

CONCLUSION

In addition to having the potential for selecting a "wrong winner" and causing other forms of political mischief, the electoral college is inherently flawed as a democratic institution because it makes some people's votes more important than others. Depending upon where a person lives, his or her vote might have enormous importance, only modest importance, or it might have no impact at all. The electoral college is biased in favor of voters in very small states and very large states. It is biased against voters in high-turnout states as compared to voters in low-turnout states. In addition, the electoral college magnifies the political power of some strategically located and well-organized groups, and diminishes the importance of the votes of other groups of similar size, even going so far as to effectively disenfranchise some groups altogether. And, as we shall see in Chapter 5, the electoral college system also leads to a serious distortion of the meaning of election outcomes and their political implications.

NOTES

1. The bonus states include: the ten states in Table 3.1, plus: Arkansas (+1), Colorado (+1), Connecticut (+1), Hawaii (+2), Idaho (+2), Iowa

(+1), Kansas (+1), Maine (+1), Mississippi (+1), Nebraska (+1), New Mexico (+2), Oklahoma (+1), Rhode Island (+2), South Carolina (+1), Utah (+2), and West Virginia (+1).

2. The states that were penalized are the ten largest states, (Table 3.2) plus: Arizona (-1), Georgia (-1), Indiana (-1), Massachusetts (-1), Missouri (-1), Oregon (-1), and Virginia (-1).

3. The states that got their "fair share" in the 1980s are: Alabama, Kentucky, Louisiana, Maryland, Minnesota, Tennessee, Washington, and Wisconsin.

4. See John F. Banzhaf, III, "One Man, 3312 Votes: A Mathematical Analysis of the Electoral College," *Villanova Law Review* 13 (Winter 1968) pp. 303–46, and John H. Yunker and Lawrence D. Longley, "The Biases of the Electoral College: Who Really is Advantaged?" in Donald R. Matthews, ed. *Perspectives on Presidential Selection* (Washington, D.C.: Brookings Institution, 1973), pp. 172–203. See also Lawrence D. Longley and James D. Dana, "New Empirical Estimates of the Electoral College for the 1980s," *Western Political Quarterly* 37 (March 1984), pp. 157–75, and George Rabinowitz and Stuart Elaine MacDonald, "The Power of the States in U.S. Presidential Elections," *American Political Science Review* 80 (March 1986), pp. 65–87. Two thorough and readable overviews of the research on state vote power biases are found in Neal R. Peirce and Lawrence D. Longley, *The People's President: The Electoral College in American History and the Direct Vote Alternative*, rev. ed. (New Haven, Conn.: Yale University Press, 1981), pp. 119–25, and William R. Keech, "Background Paper" in *Winner Take All: Report of the Twentieth Century Fund Task Force on Reform of the Presidential Selection Process* (New York: Holmes and Meier Publishers, 1978), pp. 27–33.

5. Emeritus Prof. Paul Freund of Harvard Law School in testimony before the Senate Judiciary Committee, July 28, 1977.

6. C. Herman Pritchett, *The American Constitution*, 3d ed. (New York: McGraw-Hill, 1977), pp. 222–23. Judith Best minimizes the significance of this effect in her book *The Case Against the Direct Election of the President* (Ithaca, N.Y.: Cornell University Press, 1971), pp. 126–28.

7. Harvey Zeidenstein, *Direct Election of the President* (Lexington, Mass.: D. C. Heath, 1973), pp. 5–6.

8. Ibid., p. 11.

9. Mark Levy and Michael Kramer, *The Ethnic Factor* (New York: Simon and Schuster, 1973), pp. 226, 240–44.

10. Yunker and Longley, "The Biases of the Electoral College," pp. 191–92.

11. These commercials attacked Gov. Dukakis because a Black convicted murderer had committed an interracial rape while on furlough from a

Massachusetts prison. The ads featured Horton's picture, making the racial implications unmistakable.

12. Estimates of the number of Jews vary from about 5 million to about 6 million. There are about 4 million Mormons.

5

Distorted Election Interpretations

Lopsided popular vote victories are rare in American presidential elections; landslides are rarer; and obliterations of the loser do not occur. The average popular vote percentage received by winning candidates in the twentieth century was only 53.9; in the last century winners did even worse, averaging only 49.6 percent of the popular vote. The largest victory in American history was Lyndon Johnson's in 1964 when he received 61 percent of the total vote to Barry Goldwater's 39 percent. Other big winners also lost sizable portions of the vote: approximately 40 percent of the electorate did not vote for Calvin Coolidge in 1924, Franklin D. Roosevelt in 1936, and Richard Nixon in 1972. All in all, presidential elections in this country have been quite competitive.

But you would never know that if you looked at electoral vote counts, because they have usually magnified the gap between winner and loser. The electoral college system produces strange anomalies: winners squeak in at the polls but capture the lion's share of the electoral votes; losers do quite well but get a relatively small yield in electoral votes; third parties who make a dent in the popular vote usually get nothing by way of electoral votes in return. The process of converting state-by-state voting returns into electoral votes produces distorted results, and such misrepresentations have all kinds of political ramifications. This chapter examines these distortions and their consequences.

MAGNIFIED MAJORITIES

Table 5.1 illustrates the gap between winners' electoral and popular votes in elections since 1920. The distance between the two outcomes in each year shows that the winning candidate normally has had his margin of success exaggerated in the electoral college. The "bonus" obtained by the winner is most significant when the candidate wins by a comfortable margin at the polls but then sees his measured victory register as a virtual wipe-out of the loser in the electoral college. It is our familiar winner-take-all principle that is again responsible because the winning candidate of a state gets all of its electoral votes even if the margin of victory was very narrow. The losing candidate in each state gets nothing; the winner gets everything; and the result can be an enormous inflation of the winner's margin.

Identifying winners of the elections listed in Table 5.1 makes this point clearer. Hoover got 58 percent of the popular vote in 1928 but a hefty 84 percent of the electoral vote. Roosevelt did win big when he ran for reelection in 1936, but the 98 percent of the electoral vote he received was way out of proportion to the 61 percent he got at the polls. Nixon in 1972 benefited similarly, seeing his 61 percent of the popular vote soar to 97 percent of the electoral vote. And Ronald Reagan twice was helped by the magnification effect: in 1980 he barely got a majority of the popular vote (50.7 percent), but he got 91 percent of the electors; gaining 59 percent of the popular vote in 1984 enabled him to win the electoral college vote almost unanimously, receiving an astounding 98 percent of the vote. Substantial division in the electorate is masked when winners such as these corner the market on electoral votes.

This potential for inflating the dimensions of victory via the electoral college can produce peculiar ironies. Jimmy Carter in 1976 won 50.1 percent of the popular vote when he ousted Gerald

Table 5.1
The Gap Between Presidents' Electoral and Popular Vote Percentages: 1920-1988

Year	Presidents' Electoral Vote Percentage	Presidents' Popular Vote Percentage	"The Gap"
1920	76%	60%	16%
1924	72	54	18
1928	84	58	26
1932	89	57	32
1936	98	61	37
1940	85	55	30
1944	81	53	28
1948	57	50	7
1952	83	55	28
1956	86	57	29
1960	56	50	6
1964	90	61	29
1968	56	43	13
1972	97	61	36
1976	55	50	5
1980	91	51	40
1984	98	59	39
1988	79	54	25
MEAN (1920-1988)	80%	55%	25%

Ford from the presidency. Four years later Ronald Reagan unseated Carter with only slightly more popular votes—50.7 percent of the total. But while Carter's votes yielded him only 297 electoral votes, Reagan's produced 489 electoral votes. Carter's victory looks very slim (which in fact it was since it is the electoral college that is decisive), whereas Reagan's comes out as a romp. This is electoral college magic: the augmentation of a meager win into a thundering triumph.

Such prestidigitation can also make presidents who got less than half of the vote look as if they are the choice of the majority. Five times in the twentieth century winning candidates could not command a majority at the polls, but they were able to muster over 50 percent in the electoral college and therefore win the presidency. The most glaring transformation of modest popular appeal into overwhelming electoral college strength occurred in 1912 when Woodrow Wilson won 42 percent of the popular vote and got 82 percent of the electoral votes. This was a three-man election, and Wilson was able to pick up most of the electoral votes when Republican William Howard Taft and Republican-defector Theodore Roosevelt running as the Progressive Party candidate split the anti-Wilson vote. Wilson snuck into the presidency with two-fifths of the vote, but there was no contest in the electoral college; he won hands down. All it takes in any state is a plurality to win all that state's electoral votes, so lots of submajority finishes can nevertheless produce substantial yields of electoral votes.

The other side of the coin is the sad situation facing losers. Those who have succeeded in gaining the allegiance of vast multitudes often get nearly shut out when the electoral votes are counted. These "also-rans" become historical footnotes and sometimes even laughingstocks, despite the fact that they really fared pretty well at the polls. It is quite a list: Michael Dukakis, who got 46 percent of the popular vote in 1988, but only 21 percent of the electoral vote; Walter Mondale, recipient of 41 percent of the popular vote in 1984 but a measly two percent of the electoral vote; George McGovern, the favorite of 38 percent of the electorate in 1972, who only managed to salvage three percent of the electoral vote; and (to show that Republicans can suffer the same ignominious fate) Barry Goldwater who got 38 percent of the vote in 1964 but a scant 10 percent of the electors. The electoral college can make credible candidates look like total rejects.

In a nutshell, the electoral college has been much kinder to winning presidential candidates than the voters have been. To repeat, this is a result of the rules of the game. Win 50.1 percent of the voters in a state, or even less if there are more than two candidates, and you bask in the riches of the entire complement of that state's electoral votes. And if your support is sufficiently broad nationally to enable you to finish first in many states, you are able to vanquish your rival in the electoral college despite having accomplished the narrowest of victories in a good many places. The system (miraculously) has not produced many wrong winners, but it sure has produced a good number of "photo-finish" winners who wind up appearing much stronger politically than they really are.

ILLUSIONS OF LANDSLIDES

It is a familiar election-night ritual every four years. Network television reporting begins with the closing of the polls in the East, and the focal point of such coverage is "the map." A color is assigned to each candidate, and as soon as a winner is declared in each state the map is coded accordingly. Before long, the map gets filled in and the nation gets to see a national electoral portrait. In the days to come, newspapers and news magazines reproduce the same picture.

But these representations can be quite misleading. A perfect example is the 1988 two-color map that appeared in *Time* in which states won by Republican Bush are blue and states won by Democrat Dukakis are red.[1] What immediately strikes the reader is the broad swatch of blue that covers almost the entire country, indicating the great number of states where Bush was victorious. A glimpse at this map implies that Dukakis' share of the vote was puny and that he was utterly trounced by his opponent. And as if the sheer geographic portrayal were not enough, it is superimposed on a backdrop of a gigantic elephant (the symbol of the Republican Party) standing next to a barely visible little donkey representing the Democratic Party showing.

This symbolism is very misleading on two separate counts. First, the physical size of states has no relationship to the number of people living in them and the number of votes cast in them. Thus in 1988 the ten mountain and plains states won by Bush take up a very large part of the map (Nevada, Utah, Idaho, Montana, Wyoming, Colorado, Kansas, Nebraska, South Dakota, and North Dakota). But relatively few people live there; the population of all these states is about 11 million in contrast to the single state of New York, whose population is nearly 18 million. Seven times as many people live in Massachusetts, barely visible on the map, as live in gigantic Montana. As a result of this distortion, Dukakis' victories in New York and Massachusetts pale in comparison with Bush's victories in the West despite the fact that Dukakis garnered far more popular votes in these two states than Bush secured in the ten mountain and plains states that comprise so much of the map. Maps represent acres, but acres do not vote; people do.

The second problem arising from the standard map portrayal of election results is the winner-take-all aspect of the electoral college, which visually makes it look as if the loser got no votes in the states he or she lost. To be sure, Bush received nationwide support in 1988; he won all but eleven states and the District of Columbia enabling him to muster up 426 electoral votes (80 percent of the total). But camouflaged in such visual imagery is the closeness of the vote; Dukakis gave Bush a run for the money. In a campaign that saw Bush at first successfully label his adversary as an out-of-the-mainstream liberal who was soft on crime and low on patriotism, Dukakis came storming back at the end by appealing to traditional Democratic Party values. It was not quite a photo-finish, but the two candidates finished only *eight percentage points* apart: Bush received 54 percent of the vote to Dukakis' 46 percent. The reality so misrepresented by the map is that the country was almost equally divided in its presidential preference.

Walter Mondale, the loser to Reagan in 1984, was even more seriously victimized by the map affliction. Recall that he received 41 percent of the popular vote, but his showing is hardly visible in an electoral college depiction of the results. Because he won only one state and the District of Columbia, he is virtually "wiped off the map." It is not that the maps are inaccurate; it is that they caricature the results by making it seem that the losers were completely shut out in most states whereas in fact they were piling up millions of votes.

Whereas the maps distort voting behavior pictorially, reporting of the electoral vote numbers distorts results arithmetically. It is commonplace to hear the electoral vote "score": Bush's 426 to Dukakis' 111, Reagan's 525 to Mondale's 13, Reagan's 489 to Carter's 49. Partially because large numbers are so cumbersome, it is rare that the distribution of the raw votes come to light. No one speaks of Bush's 48,881,278 to Dukakis' 41,805,374 or Reagan's 54,455,075 to Mondale's 37,577,185.

The central problem with using electoral vote maps and tallies to characterize election results is the magnification effect (for winners) and the minimization effect (for losers) caused by the electoral college system. Astute vote-watchers are not misled by electoral vote counts and maps. But in fact many are taken in by such descriptions, which come to assume a reality of their own.

The media succumbs to and perpetuates such fallacious thinking in the process of describing and interpreting election results. For the many who are not interested in delving into the details of the vote because they are too busy, too bored, too disgusted, or just plain apathetic, news headlines and lead sentences are critical conveyors of information. And such "quick reads" of the election often reflect electoral college outcomes rather than the popular vote.

Thus in 1980, when Reagan received only 51 percent of the popular vote, the national news magazines trumpeted his victory as almost the second coming. With electoral vote maps glowing in vivid colors, *Time* minced no words in characterizing the outcome: "Landslide. Yes, landslide—stunning, startling, astounding, beyond the wildest dreams and nightmares of the contending camps, beyond the furthest ken of armies of pollsters, pundits and political professionals."[2] *Newsweek* too used the map to portray a "landslide of stunning dimension."[3]

Even the normally stolid *Washington Post* got embroiled in landslide-mania. Its lead story the day after the election bannered "Reagan Sweeps to a Landslide Victory."[4] The article, written by David Broder, emphasized Reagan's sweeping victory in the electoral college. Not until the seventh paragraph is mention made of the fact that Reagan got about 50 percent of the vote, the same as the combined tally of his two opponents.

The dubious nature of much of the reporting was noted by the *New York Times* in its editorial two days after the election.[5] Somewhat sardonically, it commented that Reagan's victory was *not* a landslide. It went on to explain how the electoral vote vastly magnifies the popular vote and therefore needs to be interpreted very cautiously. This advice is correct—but rarely heeded.

Thus, the lengthy *Time* analysis following the 1988 election is entitled "Color It Republican." In the first paragraph we are told of a "decisive victory" and a "mini-landslide."[6] *Newsweek* echoed the same theme: "When the ballots rolled in, it was very nearly a landslide." They too made "the map" the centerpiece of their article; it was headlined "A Blowout in the Electoral College" and described Bush's victory there as "a rout."[7]

It is not so much that the above headlines and copy are wrong; they are literally correct. It is that they represent the electoral vote as something it is *not*—an expression of popular will. "*Decisive* victory"? "Nearly a *landslide*"? Perhaps, if the focus is on Bush's ability to commandeer 426 out of 538 electoral votes; but sheer nonsense if we bear in mind that loser Dukakis got 46 percent of the vote. Journalism stresses the map metaphor and in so doing fosters myths about voter consensus that did not exist.

Even scholars occasionally fall prey to "map-itis." In a highly respected analysis of the election of 1980 written by political scientists (complete with an electoral college map), the article describing the outcome begins with the following sentence: "The results were clear: Ronald Reagan was decisively elected President on November 4, 1980."[8] We are first told of his victory in forty-four out of the fifty states that netted him 489 electoral votes out of a possible 538. Next comes a litany of places where Reagan came in first: "liberal Massachusetts, economically depressed Michigan, booming Texas, traditionalist Utah, and contemporary California."[9] Finally, mention of the popular vote: "Of the 86 million Americans who cast their ballots, the Republican candidate won a clear majority."[10]

While these statements are literally true, they are grossly misleading. Thus, in the interest of real accuracy, the statement made earlier should have read: "Of the 86 million Americans who cast their ballots, the Republican candidate won a bare majority (50.7 percent)." Why did the author choose to ignore the fact that nearly half of the voters had voted for other candidates? We would suggest that he was "sucked in" by the magnitude of the electoral college so much that he minimized the strength of the anti-Reagan vote.

So misleading descriptions of the vote and questionable interpretations abound. In Chapter 2 we saw how the electoral college can make winners out of losers. Here we see how it can turn unspectacular victories at the polls into apparent landslides. The distance between winners and losers in presidential election battles is rarely as great as it is made to appear.

FALSE MANDATES

You may be wondering: What is so upsetting about losers getting "short-changed" in the electoral college? What difference does it make if the winner's total is usually exaggerated? What's all the shouting about? A win is a win is a win; a loss is a loss is a loss.

The answers lie in the way results are interpreted, and the impact of such interpretations on subsequent political behavior. Election outcomes are a source of political ammunition for those in office as well as a source of guidance to them. The fanfare of campaigns and vote-counting dies quickly, but the elections live on to influence what politicians do. The phenomenon of magnified victories produced by the workings of the electoral college has long-run political consequences.

There are some positive effects. First, the illusion of "sweeps" legitimates the results of the election. Bitter campaigns leave battle scars, and those voting against presidents-elect are sometimes loathe to accept their authority. Puffing up the size of the president-elect's victory may make him or her seem more like the "people's choice," perhaps more likely to get the respect if not the loyalty of those who voted for the other party's candidate.[11]

A second benefit ensuing from the magnification effect of electoral college voting is presidential empowerment. Presidential power is a sometimes thing; it does not come automatically with the office. In order to get their programs adopted by a resisting Congress and to have their policies implemented by a sometimes recalcitrant federal bureaucracy, presidents often rely on their nationwide popularity as an arm-twisting device. Presidential power has been described by one authority as the "power to persuade,"[12] and the appearance of having been swept into office can win over dissidents.

However, the negative consequences of such empowerment may outweigh the benefits. First of all, the ballooning of the dimensions of a president's victory may enable him or her to push through political agendas that are opposed by the majority. The inaccurate appearance of near-consensus fostered by such magnification may provide considerable impetus for approval of measures that are lacking in far-reaching public support.

Certainly Ronald Reagan was helped in getting his big tax cuts favoring the rich and spending cuts hurting the poor through the Congress by the false mandate arising from his electoral college rout of Jimmy Carter and John Anderson. He looked like a big winner and was hailed as such even though he only won the slimmest of majorities at the polls. The 1980 election results were far different than they appeared: 49.3 percent of the voters did not vote for Reagan; 50 percent of eligible voters did not vote at all; and Reagan thus received votes from only about 26 percent of the eligible electorate. And if we also take into account the many Democrats who voted for Reagan mainly as a rejection of Carter's ineffectiveness, it seems very doubtful that there was anything approaching majority support for his inegalitarian policies. But his much-touted "landslide," more illusion than reality, no doubt bolstered his power in dealing with Congress.

Similar benefits may accrue to George Bush. Bush's percentage of the popular vote was only a bit higher than Reagan's in 1980, and, in fact, outside the South the popular vote was split fairly evenly between Bush and Michael Dukakis.[13] But winning nearly 80 percent of the electoral vote has made him a more formidable president and may well account for his success in rallying support from Congress.

Another unfortunate effect of the electoral college's inflation of the magnitude of victory is that it endows the president with excessive power. Presidents who believe that the country overwhelmingly supported them (when it did not) may be tempted to act autocratically. Basking in the glow of public adoration can lead presidents to think they can do no wrong, even if the public adoration does not exist.

So it is said that four-term President Franklin D. Roosevelt ran roughshod over those who opposed his New Deal programs. Historian Arthur Schlesinger has even said that a tradition of an "imperial presidency" started during his tenure.[14] His four victories produced popular winning percentages at the polls of 57.4, 60.8, 54.7, and 53.4 percent; but his ability to carry most of the states in all four elections produced electoral vote majorities of 88.9, 98.5, 84.6, and 81.4 percent. The impressiveness of the latter sets of figures, doubtlessly contributing to the erroneous image of Roosevelt as the "people's president," may well have encouraged Roosevelt to seek too much power and prompted the nation to give him what he wanted.

Finally, distorted results have impacts on losers, their supporters, and their parties. The illusion of having been wiped out in the presidential election even when their candidate did fairly well can be demoralizing. Thus, Blacks in the 1980s may well have felt totally outside the national political spectrum as they were constantly reminded that Republican candidates for whom they had little use were "landslide" victors. Losing is losing, but the electoral college results really rub it in.

ECLIPSED PROTEST VOTES

The electoral college creates a strange paradox. Third parties receive abnormally high clout in close elections as was explained in the last chapter. If the electoral votes are more or less evenly divided, they can hold the balance of power in the electoral college or shunt the election into the House of Representatives. The electoral college enhances their opportunity to be spoilers, because small numbers of popular votes going to them can cost one of the major parties the entire electoral vote of a state.

However, under other circumstances their influence is diluted. They may get a respectable number of votes at the polls throughout the nation, but because they do not come out ahead in any state, they receive no electoral college votes. In the twentieth century, an average of 5.2 percent of the voters rejected the two major parties at the polls each election and cast their votes otherwise, but the average electoral vote produced by such defections was only 1.0 percent. Consequently, their supporters who are dissatisfied with major party choices have virtually *no* impact on the vote count that counts—the mighty electoral college.

Some elections, featuring substantial voter disaffection with the two major parties, have resulted in substantial electoral vote deficits suffered by third parties. Thus in 1924 Robert La Follette's Progressive Party got only the 13 electoral votes from his home state of Wisconsin instead of the 91 he would have been entitled to on the basis of receiving 17.1 percent of the national popular vote. La Follette not only appealed to discontented farmers and railroad workers angry about their experience of anti-union repression, but he drew support from millions dissatisfied with the choice between a conservative Republican (Calvin Coolidge) and a conservative Democrat (corporation lawyer John W. Davis). This was a broad-based candidacy: La Follette received nearly 5 million votes, winning over 20 percent of the vote in ten states, over 30 percent in eight states, and over 40 percent in three states. But the significance of this quite sizable protest vote was almost totally eclipsed in the electoral college tally, and the liberal causes favored by these voters such as the right of labor to form unions were put on the back burner until Franklin Roosevelt was elected eight years later.

Representative John Anderson's showing in 1980 was in some ways even more remarkable. Whereas La Follette had played a major role in the U.S. Senate for two decades, Anderson emerged from obscurity as an Illinois congressman to battle Democratic President Jimmy Carter and Republican challenger Ronald Reagan. His Independent Party, a bootstrap operation lacking national organizational structure and a steady flow of funds, nevertheless received 6.6 percent of the popular vote. Many voters opted for a candidate lacking in both experience and charisma out of dismay with the choice between a too-conservative Reagan and a seemingly ineffectual Carter whose handling of the Iran hostage crisis drew such voter ire. And another 1.7 percent voted for even lesser-known fourth and fifth party candidates, bringing the total vote against the two major parties to 8.3 percent.

Anderson did very well, but you would never know it from the electoral vote count; he got nothing for his efforts. A solid nationwide protest vote coming almost equally from Democrats and Republicans[15] was generally dismissed as a sideshow in the campaign due to Anderson's winning no states and getting *zero* electoral votes. Anderson's loss was Reagan's gain: The mythology of a Reagan landslide discussed earlier was in no small part created by this eclipse of the third-party vote in the electoral college.

Votes for third parties ordinarily reflect protest against the conventional policies of the "establishment" parties or a revolt against the ideological choices that they offer. While most third parties tend to be ephemeral, at particular points of time they serve as divining rods for tapping resentment against current directions of American politics. And during particularly turbulent periods they can register considerable success at the polls, success that is usually eradicated when the electoral votes are counted. Under some circumstances, third parties can play a decisive role, but the electoral college normally consigns them to oblivion.

CONCLUSION

So how the votes are counted has political ramifications, for better and (mainly) for worse. Winners are emboldened; losers are belittled. The magnification effect is basically undemocratic; it contributes to a misrepresentation of the body politic. The votes in the electoral college, plain and simply, misrepresent the voters' decision.

NOTES

1. "Anatomy of a Disaster," *Time*, November 21, 1988, p. 33.
2. "Reagan Coast-to-Coast," *Time*, November 17, 1980, p. 22.
3. "The Republican Landslide," *Newsweek*, November 17, 1980, p. 28.
4. David Broder, "Reagan Sweeps to a Landslide Victory," *The Washington Post*, November 5, 1980, p. A1.
5. "The November Surprises," *The New York Times*, November 6, 1980, p. A34.
6. "Color It Republican," *Time*, November 21, 1988, p. 32.
7. "The Tough Tasks Ahead," *Newsweek*, November 21, 1988, p. 9.
8. Gerald Pomper, "The Presidential Election," in idem et al. *The Election of 1980: Reports and Interpretations* (Chatham, N.J.: Chatham House Publishers, 1981), p. 65.
9. Ibid., p. 67.
10. Ibid.
11. This is the argument of Paul Perkins in favor of the winner-take-all principle. Says Perkins, "The Electoral College works because it expresses the will of the people in a way that tends to widen the margin of the winner and thus defuse the disruptive potential of the transition of power." See his "What's Good about the Electoral College," *Washington Monthly* 9 (April 1977), pp. 40–41.
12. Richard Neustadt, *Presidential Power: The Politics of Leadership* (New York: John Wiley, 1962), chap. 3.

13. E. J. Dionne, Jr., "Bush Is Elected by 6-5 Margin with Solid GOP Base in South; Democrats Hold Both Houses," *The New York Times*, November 9, 1988, p. A1.

14. Arthur Schlesinger, *The Imperial Presidency* (Boston: Houghton-Mifflin, 1973).

15. Paul Abramson, John Aldrich, and David Rohde, *Change and Continuity in the 1980 Elections* (Washington, D.C.: Congressional Quarterly Press, 1982), pp. 172–84.

6

Letting the People Decide

The year was 1796. Recall from Chapter 1 that Federalist John Adams had been elected president in the electoral college to succeed George Washington, but his opponent, anti-Federalist Thomas Jefferson, was elected vice president. What had happened was that under the double-balloting scheme of the original Constitution, Jefferson had received *more* votes than Adams's running mate, Thomas Pinckney, because a few electors who voted for Adams refused to vote for Pinckney. The Constitution had misfired.

But the worst was yet to come. Four years later in 1800 Jefferson again ran against Adams, who was seeking reelection. Jefferson won, but when the electoral votes were counted, he wound up with the exact number of votes as his own party's candidate for vice president, Aaron Burr. The fact that no one defected from the party's vice presidential choice (as had happened in 1796) almost did Jefferson in, because the Constitution provided that if the electoral votes were tied, the House of Representatives was to choose the president. They chose Jefferson, but it took an entire week of political machinations and thirty-six ballots to do so. Again, a flaw in the mechanisms of the electoral college had created political chaos.

So after only four presidential elections had been held it had become clear that the nation faced a "pick your poison" situation stemming from the double-balloting procedure of Article II. If electors were loyal to their political party and cast both their ballots for the party's presidential and vice presidential choices, a tie vote was inevitable and the selection of the president would wind up in the House of Representatives, where all kinds of scheming could take place. On the other hand, if some electors abandoned their party's vice presidential choice the opponent's presidential candidate might well get second place in the voting and become vice president. In short, the country found itself in one big constitutional mess.

What occurred next was a proud moment in American history. The nation's leaders realized that the presidential election machinery was not working properly and that there was only one sensible thing to do: fix it. The Twelfth Amendment to the Constitution was proposed abolishing the simultaneous double-balloting procedure and replacing it with the current arrangement whereby electors cast two separate ballots—one for president and one for vice president. Despite considerable opposition from small states reluctant to reduce the role of the House of Representatives where they would have more power due to the one state-one vote arrangement, the amendment passed both houses of Congress in 1803 and was quickly ratified in 1804—in time for the next election. Partisan and narrow state interests were overcome by appeals to a broader national interest in avoiding the kinds of fiascos that occurred in 1796 and 1800. Never again would we see the bizarre situation of a partisan division between presidents and vice presidents in the same administration or the equally perverse scenario of the House of Representatives flirting with the idea of switching around the winning party's presidential and vice presidential candidates because the two happened to wind up in a tie.

However, more fundamental defects in our presidential selection method remained. The Twelfth Amendment cured a technical infirmity of the electoral college but left untouched the more serious maladies occasioned by indirect election of the presidency that have been described in the preceding chapters. If our early politicians could alter the Constitution after only fifteen years of bad experiences with it, surely the accumulated wisdom of the next 185 years ought to be sufficient impetus to spur more dramatic changes that strike at the roots of a woefully deficient system. It is time for the founder's folly to be undone.

MODIFYING THE ELECTORAL COLLEGE

In the first half of the eighteenth century, the states went a long way in the direction of democratizing the presidential selection system. The Constitution permits them to choose their electors in any manner they see fit, and at the outset of the republic a variety of methods were used, including selection by the state legislature. But by 1868 the states had moved to the current system of popular voting for electors on a winner-take-all basis. States have been reluctant to change unilaterally to a fairer system of dividing votes between winning and losing candidates for fear that giving up its bloc vote would reduce the state's power to influence the outcome in the electoral college and diminish the appeals that candidates would make to the states. Consequently, with the exception of Maine, which has adopted a district system (described below), states have made only very minor changes in their procedures for picking electors.

Given the reluctance of the states to change their procedures, the main focus of attempts to change presidential election rules has been in Congress through the constitutional amendment process. Well over five hundred proposals, dating back to 1797, have been introduced to change the system; all have failed (apart from the Twelfth Amendment). A staggering variety of changes have been proposed to remedy some of the problems of the electoral college, but most of them fall into three categories: automaticity, proportionality, and the district plan. And as we shall now see, these efforts involve tinkering with the election machinery rather than overhaul. None of them are worthwhile.

Automaticity

Those becoming acquainted with the workings of the electoral college are often horrified to learn that it is perfectly legitimate for electors to vote for whomever they please regardless of the balloting of the voters. It is frequently asked: What is to prevent an elector from voting for the losing candidate or for someone who was not even on the ballot? The answer: absolutely nothing.

This is the problem of the so-called faithless elector who acts autonomously and defies the voting of the electorate. It is not just a hypothetical possibility; some electors have indeed gone their own way. In 1972, a Republican elector from Virginia voted for John Hospers, the Libertarian Party candidate for president (who received only 3,673 votes *nationwide*); in 1976 a Washington elector voted for Ronald Reagan instead of Gerald Ford (four years before Reagan was the Republican nominee); and in 1988 a Democratic West Virginia elector cast her vote for Democratic vice presidential candidate Lloyd Bentsen rather than vote for Democratic standardbearer Michael Dukakis for president. These electors were well within their constitutional rights and indeed could have voted for anyone they pleased: Bill Cosby, Ollie North, Joe Montana, Barbara Walters—or Mickey Mouse.

Automaticity is meant to deal with this contingency. It is a fancy word with a simple meaning: All of the electoral votes of a state would be automatically assigned to the candidate who won the most popular votes in that state. Under some versions, electors would cease to be real people and their votes would be recorded in the electoral college strictly on the basis of how the state voted. In alternative plans (which sixteen states have adopted on their own), electors are forced to vote for the candidate to which they were pledged. If the Democratic slate of electors is chosen (because the Democratic candidate comes out ahead), electors *must* vote for the Democrat. Either way, the elector as an independent actor would be eliminated and the outcome of the electoral college could be determined for certain as soon as all the popular votes are counted.

These plans are all well and good, but they deal with a trivial problem. The issue of the faithless elector is a tempest in a teapot, a "red herring" deflecting attention away from more serious matters. Of the 18,473 electors who cast votes between 1820 and 1988, only eight acted contrary to the way they were supposed to vote, and none of these erratic votes came even close to having a bearing on the outcome. In other words, in well over 999 cases out of 1,000, electors have been faith*ful* rather than faith*less*.

This is not surprising. Electors are relatively unknown people who have been chosen mainly because of their service and loyalty to their political party. A 1968 elector baldly acknowledged his own unimportance: "My finest credentials were that each year I contributed what money I could to the party."[1] Folks such as these are unlikely to be mavericks; fidelity to their party is their stock in trade. They are usually solid and dependable politicos drawn from the party's mainstream who will almost always do what is expected of them—which means carrying out the will of the voters of their state. Insofar as the automatic elector plan is directed at them, it is aiming at a problem that does not exist.

There is one benefit that might accrue from automaticity. Given the system as it is, in the case of an impending tie or near-tie in the electoral college something weird could happen. Either as a result of bribery or because the elector is ideologically disgruntled with his or her own party's standardbearer, he or she might cross over to the other party's candidate. In a case when a third party candidate secures enough electors to deny either major party, some electors of one major party might cross over to the other to prevent the election from being thrown into the House. Automatic balloting by electors would prevent any such irregular and idiosyncratic behavior on the part of electors from determining presidential outcomes.

This slight benefit is insufficient to make the automatic plan worthwhile. The harm of automaticity is not what it would accomplish but what it would *not* accomplish. Getting rid of potentially defiant electors would make it appear as if a constitutional dragon had been slain when in fact that monster would still be on the loose. Wrong winners could still prevail; the House of Representatives would still have an altogether unpredictable role; the bias against certain states and interests would go uncorrected; and electoral vote outcomes would remain distortions of the electorate's behavior. In the words of Birch Bayh, the twentieth century's leading advocate of electoral college reform who opposed automaticity: "Mere procedural changes in the present system would be like shifting around the parts of a creaky and dangerous automobile engine, making it no less creaky and no less dangerous. What we may need is a whole new engine."[2] Bayh was right: Automaticity is a charade giving the illusion of significant improvement while in reality preserving the status quo.

Proportionality

This plan would allocate the electoral votes of each state according to the breakdown of the popular votes in each state. In order to make the distribution of the electoral votes closely proportionate to the popular vote results in each state, each electoral vote would be broken up into thousandths. The system would dispense with real human beings serving as electors since people obviously cannot be divided up into fractions.

Let us illustrate proportionality by figuring out the distribution of California's 47 electoral votes in 1988. Bush received 51.1 percent of the popular vote in that state to Dukakis's 47.6 percent; the remaining 1.3 percent went to other candidates. To calculate Bush's electoral votes, we multiply .511 (which is the same as 51.1 percent) times 47 giving him 24.029; likewise, Dukakis gets .476 times 47 or 22.353 electoral votes; the left over .618 is sprinkled among the assemblage of minor candidates.

The major appeal of this plan is that it seems to reduce wrong-winner possibilities. By getting rid of the winner-take-all feature of the current arrangement, it does away with wasted votes. A candidate's big margin of victory in any state pays off in extra electoral votes. On the other side of the coin, losers get consolation prizes—often good-sized packages of electoral votes depending on how close to victory in a state they came. Close popular vote outcomes result in close electoral vote outcomes, so there is no unfair bonus going to candidates who squeak to victory in a particular state, who currently reap a bonanza of the state's entire package of electoral votes.

A two-state example from 1988 illustrated in Table 6.1 makes this clear. Compare the outcomes in Utah and West Virginia, and it will be readily recognized as the classic wrong-winner paradigm explained in Chapter 2. Bush slaughters Dukakis in Utah, getting all five of the state's electoral votes. Dukakis barely edges out Bush in West Virginia but nevertheless also gets all six electoral votes. So despite the fact that Bush has received 190,139 more popular votes than Dukakis in the two states, Dukakis comes out ahead in electoral votes.

Table 6.2 shows what would happen in the same two states under the proportional plan.

Notice that the wrong-winner outcome disappears. Dukakis loses the bonus he gets under the current state of affairs; Bush is no longer deprived of the benefit of his landslide in Utah. Consequently, Bush not only gets more electoral votes than Dukakis; he gets substantially more, reflecting the fact that his popular vote totals in the two states were so much greater than Dukakis's. Proportionality has rectified things: the "right winner" wins.

So far, so good. It looks as if the possibility of a wrong-winner disaster has been obviated by proportionality. Not so! Because of the malapportionment of electors among the states discussed in Chapter 4, candidates could still get electoral votes disproportionate to the number of votes they secured at the polls. Two problems, both of which stem from the unfair allocation of electoral votes, account for the counterintuitive possibility of wrong winners under proportionality.

First, the small-state bias would give the popular vote winner in such states more electoral votes than are deserved, and it would shortchange the winners in larger states. Recall from Table 4.4

Table 6.1
Allocation of Electoral Votes in Two States Under Current Rules

	Popular Vote		Electoral Vote	
	Bush	Dukakis	Bush	Dukakis
Utah	428,442	207,352	5	0
West Virginia	310,065	341,016	0	6
TOTAL	738,507	548,368	5	6

Table 6.2
Allocation of Electoral Votes Under Proportionality

	Bush	Dukakis
Utah	3.311	1.602
West Virginia	2.848	3.132
TOTAL	6.159	4.734

that California in the 1980s got 47 electoral votes but was entitled to 56 based on population; the District of Columbia got three electoral votes but should only have gotten one. So under proportionality Dukakis, who won the District in 1988 with 83 percent of the vote would get .83 times 3 or 2.49 electoral votes, but he would only deserve .83 times 1 or 0.83. Bush, who carried 52 percent of California's vote in 1988 would get .52 times 47 or 24.4 electoral votes whereas he ought to receive .52 times 56 or 28.1 electoral votes. Thus, a candidate whose strength is preponderantly in smaller states would get an edge under the proportional plan while a candidate whose victories are concentrated in larger states would lose out. In a close election, these inequities could reward the popular vote loser with sufficient unwarranted electoral votes to make him or her the winner in the electoral college.

The second problem has its root in the turnout bias. Smashing victories in states with high voter turnout would not be adequately reflected in electoral votes because electoral votes are assigned primarily on the basis of a state's population rather than the number of people going to the polls. Even under proportionality, popular votes in high-turnout states would get discounted and popular votes in low-turnout states would get inflated—thus contributing to the possibility of a wrong winner outcome.

Analysis of past election results shows that ironically enough proportionality would have created more wrong winners than the current system. It would have made Democrat William Hancock our twentieth president (instead of James Garfield); William Jennings Bryan would have become the twenty-fifth president (despite losing to William McKinley by four percentage points); and Richard Nixon would have become president eight years earlier by beating John F. Kennedy in 1960.[3] In the latter election, Nixon would have received between one-half and one full electoral vote more than Kennedy despite trailing Kennedy by 113,000 votes at the polls.[4] So proportionality fails the acid test: It does not assure victory to the people's choice for president.

It may actually make matters worse. By eliminating the magnification of the winner's margin of victory caused by the winner-take-all principle under current use, it would drastically reduce the number of electoral votes typical victors would secure. Under the proportional plan, their percentage of electoral votes would normally reflect more closely their share of the popular vote.

This fact of life under proportionality would make it far more possible for the winner to fail to get the required majority of electoral votes—resulting in the shunting of presidential selection into the House of Representatives with all the thorny political problems attendant thereto. Think about it: between 1880 and 1988 there have been nine elections where the winner failed to get 50 percent of the popular vote, including Nixon in 1968 (43.4 percent) and Kennedy in 1960 (49.7 percent). None of them would have been able to convert their victories at the polls into an electoral college majority.

Indeed, even securing a majority of the popular vote is no guarantee of getting the necessary 270 electoral votes under the proportionality plan. Jimmy Carter received 50.1 percent of the popular vote in 1976 but would have received only 269.698 electoral votes, raising the intriguing question of whether that number would have been rounded upward to the nearest whole number (giving him a majority of electoral votes on the head) or whether it would have been left as is—leaving him about three-tenths of an electoral vote shy of a majority. Even Ronald Reagan, who finished nearly ten percentage points ahead of Carter in 1980, would just barely have been elected in the electoral college with 272.922 electoral votes (only three over the magic number). Had he fallen below the 270 mark, one can only conjecture how a House of Representatives dominated by Democrats would have voted had they been entrusted with choosing among Carter, Reagan, and third-party candidate John Anderson; opportunities for political deal-making would have abounded.

The best feature of the plan is that it produces results that more closely mirror the voting of the electorate. It would destroy the illusions of landslides generated by present-day electoral college maps and provide more realistic interpretations of the voters' decision. Under proportionality, George Bush would become a modest winner in 1988 with 287.834 electoral votes—18 over a bare majority; Michael Dukakis's 244.651 electoral votes would make him a respectable loser. This would have provided a more accurate picture of what happened at the polls.

But on balance the move to proportionality would be jumping from the frying pan into the fire. Without solving the wrong-winner problem, it would compound the "no winner" problem, making the House of Representatives a probable player any time the presidential race was close or third parties with significant followings were on the scene.[5] It would lessen the power of large states by depriving them of huge chunks of electoral votes but would leave the excessive power of small states untouched. Rather than being a solution to the electoral college problem, it is a step in the wrong direction.

The District Plan

This alternative, currently used by Maine alone but previously employed by a number of states, was proposed as a mandated nationwide system as early as 1800. Each of the 435 Congressional districts would get one elector, as is currently the case, and the winning presidential candidate within each district would get that district's single electoral vote. The two electoral votes that each state would get for its two senators would be cast according to the overall outcome in the state, the winner getting both. All three of the District of Columbia's votes presumably would go to whoever won the District.

What it boils down to is this: Congressional districts would become the main arenas in which the contests for 435 electors are fought, and the states would become the sideshows where battles are waged to determine how the remaining "statewide" 100 electoral votes are cast. Only in states like Delaware that have one congressional district (and the District of Columbia) would all three of the state's electoral votes always wind up in the same candidate's electoral vote column.

Moving away from a winner-take-all system at the state level would break up the large chunks of electoral votes possessed by big states and would thus deprive such states and the interests therein of the unfair leverage they now possess in determining electoral college outcomes. No longer would a candidate like John Kennedy be able to win *all* of Illinois's 27 electoral votes by beating his opponent by a mere 8,858 votes out of nearly 5 million votes cast. There would be much less at stake in large states because large clusters of votes would no longer be up for grabs, so candidates might just as well campaign in Nevada or Rhode Island as in California or New York.

Voters favoring the minority party in noncompetitive states would regain some potential control over election of the president. Even if a state always votes for one party, there are usually one or two districts (sometimes more) where the presidential candidate of the out-party has a chance. Enclaves within states that favor the candidate who loses statewide still have a chance to score in the electoral college. All is not necessarily lost if you are a Democrat in Arizona or a Republican in Massachusetts.

The district plan permits the splitting of votes in all but the tiny states without bringing out the peril of winners being unable to gain electoral college majorities—one of the unsettling drawbacks of the proportionality system. Just as third-party candidates rarely carry whole states, so would they not be likely to carry many districts. With the two major candidates splitting all the electoral votes, the one coming out on top would always have a majority and the House of Representatives role in picking the president would be foreclosed.

So much for the positive side of the district plan; all the rest is negative. Its most crucial shortcoming is that it in fact does nothing to correct the wrong-winner perversion; it may even promote it. The plan fails because it basically follows the same winner-take-all method of allocating votes, except at the district level rather than the state level. Win a district by 50,000 votes and you get *one* electoral vote; win it by five votes and you still get *one* electoral vote.

This is the wasted vote concept all over again, but with potentially greater effects. The disparity in winning margins is much greater from district to district than from state to state, so the cumulative collection of wasted votes statewide and nationwide is likewise potentially greater than under the status quo. Because some districts are quite homogeneous (in part due to gerrymandering), winning pluralities can be enormous; but all the excess over and above a one-vote margin of victory goes down the drain. The candidate who ekes out modest victories in many districts might well win more districts (and hence more electoral votes) even though his or her opponent who piles up whopping victories in a smaller number of districts gets more popular votes altogether. Under a new guise, the wrong-winner problem reappears.

We can illustrate this problem by looking at the 1976 presidential vote breakdowns in three congressional districts in New York State (depicted in Table 6.3).[6]

Observe the wasted vote phenomenon demonstrated in the table. Carter crushed Ford in Harlem, while Ford edged out Carter in two suburban Long Island districts. The net result? Carter won the three districts by 87,278 votes, getting 34 percent more votes than Ford. But Ford would get two electoral votes under the district plan while Carter would only get one!

Broader analysis of the 1976 returns reveals just how pernicious the district plan can be. Although Carter won the entire state of New York by 288,767 votes, Ford would have received more electoral votes because he won several more districts than Carter did. The same incongruities would have occurred in Pennsylvania and Ohio: Carter won the popular vote in both states but Ford won a greater number of congressional districts.

In spite of all this, Carter apparently would still have won the 1976 election under the district plan—barely. The reason is that Carter's lost electoral votes under the district plan in states such as New York and Ohio would have been more or less offset in states such as California where Ford won the popular vote, but Carter would have won more districts and hence more electoral votes. The figures on the presidential vote breakdowns by district are inexact,[7] but it appears that Carter would have wound up with about 275 electoral votes to Ford's 263. But it would have been sheer luck that preserved Carter's victory: A few more states or districts in Ford's camp and the district plan would have made him a wrong winner.

Other elections under the district plan would have had their outcomes reversed. In 1960, John F. Kennedy faced a predica-

Table 6.3
Electoral Vote Allocation Under the District Plan: Three Selected Districts in New York

	Carter (%)	Ford (%)
4th District (Long Island)	99,242 (%)	107,420 (52)
5th District (Long Island)	111,254 (48)	118,897 (52)
16th District (Harlem)	129,187 (83)	26,088 (17)
TOTAL VOTE (three districts)	339,683 (57)	252,405 (43)

ment like that Carter would confront in 1976: huge numbers of supporters concentrated in a relative small number of districts (mainly in the central cities). He, like Carter, would have suffered from hundreds of thousands of wasted votes; but in Kennedy's case these unusable votes would have cost him the election. The district plan would have left Kennedy with 245 electoral votes to Nixon's 278 electoral votes—making Nixon a wrong winner.

The district plan, then, would be another backwards step. It continues to permit wrong-winner debacles, perhaps making them even more probable. Biases in the assignment of electors to states are worsened: The small states continue to get more than they deserve but the countervailing influence enjoyed by large states under the current system is destroyed. Third parties able to win a handful of states and districts could still do mischief by preventing either major candidate from getting a majority of electoral votes, thus throwing the election into the House of Representatives. The distortion of the popular vote would usually be lessened, but it would not be eliminated (e.g., Eisenhower, who won 57 percent of the popular vote in 1956, would have won 77 percent of the electoral votes under the district plan).

And if these failings are not enough to completely discredit the plan, there is one other consideration. The district plan would systematically help one party at the expense of the other. The Democratic Party would lose out because so many of its supporters are minority citizens packed into urban congressional districts where they produce lopsided margins of victory for presidential candidates. Such is the case, for example, of the South Side of Chicago (Illinois's First Congressional District) where for over half a century Blacks have been regularly giving Democratic presidential candidates about 90 percent of their votes. Under the district plan everything above 50 percent (currently about 100,000 votes!) would wind up as trash—wasted votes incapable of helping a Kennedy, a Carter, a Mondale, or a Dukakis win the presidency. Without much doubt, under current conditions this modification of the electoral college would function in a pro-Republican and anti-Black manner.

Although it appears at first to be an improvement over the present system, the district plan is really a wolf in sheep's clothing. It looks attractive, and as recently as 1990 some state legislatures have been considering the plan for their own states, including Connecticut and North Carolina, whose lower houses have passed bills adopting it.[8] But it is in fact an unfair and potentially disastrous method of choosing the most powerful government official in the United States. It is most assuredly *not* the way to go.

"HYBRID" PLANS

Over the years, many variations on the above schemes have been put forth to correct electoral college deficiencies while preserving the institution itself. For example, Senator Hubert H. Humphrey introduced a proposal in 1956 whereby each state would cast two electoral votes for the plurality winner in their state and the remaining electoral votes would be allocated to each candidate on the basis of his or her percentage of the national popular vote. The idea was to give to the national electorate the main voice in selecting the president but providing some separate input from the fifty state electorates. Like virtually all the so-called hybrid schemes that contain features of direct and indirect election of the president, this one was summarily rejected. It was too radical a departure for electoral college defenders and insufficiently ameliorative for electoral college critics.

One hybrid plan that did receive serious attention was the "national bonus plan" proposed by the Task Force on Reform of the Presidential Election Process assembled in the late 1970s by the Twentieth Century Fund, a foundation that sponsors policy research. The plan, explained in a book entitled *Winner Take All*,[9] would add a national pool of 102 electoral votes to the electoral college—two for each state and the District Columbia. This pool would be awarded in toto to the top national vote-getter and added to the 538 electoral votes that would continue to be allocated according to the current state-by-state winner-take-all arrangement. If no candidate received a majority of the 640 electoral votes, a second popular election would be held among the two leading candidates and the newly constituted electoral college would determine the winner.

The heart of the plan was the bonus given to the national winner, presumably enabling him or her to make up for wasted popular votes that led to a shortchanging of electoral votes; its major point was to virtually preclude the election of a wrong winner. Other advantages were elimination of the faithless elector, simplification and democratization of the contingency plan for dealing with electoral college deadlocks, and reduction of the current inequalities in voter power. And unlike direct election, it continued to preserve the power of state electorates and the dominant voting groups of which they are comprised.

The Task Force, an impressive array of experts on government including Neal Peirce, Heinz Eulau, Jeane Kirkpatrick, and Arthur Schlesinger, immediately got bogged down in conflict between those wedded to the electoral college and those wanting to scrap it. The plan, in the words of Task Force spokesman William Keech, was "plainly . . . a compromise."[10] But it was a defective compromise: Although analysis of past election returns showed that the plan would have produced no instances of popular vote winners losing in the electoral college under the bonus plan, mathematician Samuel Merrill has shown that in a close election there would remain a one-in-ten chance of a wrong winner. Merrill also demonstrated that if a third party got at least 100 electoral votes, there was a 50-50 chance that *neither* major candidate would get a majority of electoral votes.[11] On top of these shortcomings of the bonus plan, the differentials in voting power of citizens of different states would continue to be substantial.

Although the plan was introduced as a proposal for a constitutional amendment soon after it was made public, it got nowhere. One of the most prominent Task Force members, electoral college authority Neal Peirce, wrote a "partial dissent" from the final report. Said Peirce:

> I dissent, however, from the Task Force's suggestion that the national bonus plan would be preferable to simple direct election of the president. I do not believe a convincing case has been made that direct election would in any way undermine federalism, the two-party system, or the essential nature of presidential campaigns as they are now conducted.[12]

Like so many compromises, the bonus plan wound up getting the assent of almost everybody—but excited nobody. It seems destined to remain a footnote in the history of electoral college reform—and rightfully so.

DIRECT ELECTION OF THE PRESIDENT

There is only one sure way to prevent a wrong winner in the electoral college—abolish the electoral college and let the people pick the president. Under direct election, the candidate who gets the most votes nationally wins. Period.

The elegance of direct election is its simplicity. There are no complex conversions of popular votes into electoral votes, no Machiavellian strategies to win key states, no delays until an unknown body of electors ratifies the voters' choices, no waiting with bated breath to see if the election is to be thrown into the House of Representatives, no debacles or near-debacles involving an overturning of the people's choice. You just count all votes and announce the results. Winners win and losers lose.

Besides absolutely eliminating the wrong-winner specter from American politics, direct election of the president accomplishes other things. First, it equalizes voter influences on outcomes. A vote cast in Missouri becomes every bit as meaningful as a vote cast in a small state like Alaska or a huge state like California. A vote cast in a high-turnout state like Minnesota is equal to a vote cast in a low-turnout state like Mississippi. No matter what racial, ethnic, or interest group you are in, you still have the same input in the selection of the president. A vote is a vote is a vote.

Another virtue of direct election is a consequence of the first. With states no longer the battlegrounds where presidential elections are fought, campaigns might well be nationalized. People in small states especially might be given greater attention because their votes count as much in the national totals as votes from large states.

This is no minor point. Senator Hubert Humphrey, testifying in 1977 in favor of direct elections, lamented that, as the Democratic presidential candidate in 1968, he had to restrict severely his campaign itinerary. Said Humphrey:

> The large states contribute a large number of votes in the electoral college, and for this reason the campaigns are disproportionately directed toward these states. . . . In 1968, I had to make the decision as to where we would put what limited resources we had. . . . We had to ignore large sections of the country.[13]

The electoral college's effect on campaign strategy was especially well illustrated by the candidates' itineraries during the 1976 campaign.[14] Five states received more than twenty visits by the Republican and Democratic standardbearers (California, Illinois, New York, Ohio, and Pennsylvania). This is in stark contrast to the twenty-two relatively small states in each of which the combined total of all presidential and vice presidential appearances was no more than four. Under direct election, these disparities among states in candidate attention would certainly be reduced.

Another potential reshifting of candidates' appeals relates to the wasted vote phenomenon. Currently, it makes no sense for candidates to go after states where victory is either assured or hopeless. The extra votes such efforts might yield in states where a candidate is a shoo-in provide no payoff in electoral votes, and by the same token doing a little better in states that are lost causes also produces no dividend. One of the strategists in Gerald Ford's 1976 quest for reelection summed it up: "The whole thinking of the electoral college system is that those areas that you're sure to win or lose, you ignore."[15]

This would change completely under direct election. It would make just as much sense for Michael Dukakis to boost his total in Kansas by five percent, even though defeat in that state was inevitable, as to try to win votes in a state like Pennsylvania, where there was a nip-and-tuck struggle. And even though George Bush had most of the South all wrapped up from the outset of the campaign, bolstering his margin of victory would be a perfectly sound way of adding votes to his national totals. The virtual disenfranchisement of voters in noncompetitive states would end; they would regain their power to affect the ultimate decision about who becomes president.

The new state of affairs whereby *every* voter's decision could make a difference might have another positive effect: increasing the nation's woefully low voting turnout. The turnout rate of presidential elections has hovered around the 50 percent mark for years, meaning that half the eligible electorate abstains from voting. Not only does this poor showing call into question the meaningfulness of the outcome, but it undermines the authority of a newly elected president. As Table 6.4 shows, victories in our presidential elections hardly furnish a mandate because such a relatively small portion of those entitled to vote actually cast a ballot in favor of the winner. Even so-called landslide victors have only received the support of about one-third of the people.

Direct election in itself will not cause people to flock to the polls; there are many other reasons why people do not vote.[16] But it may encourage voting by people who previously had recognized that their vote did not really matter in the states where they lived. The incentive of greater efficacy might well bolster turnout and consequently increase the legitimacy of the winner's claim to be the people's choice.

Finally, the undemocratic and unpredictable role of the House of Representatives as the backup institution to elect the president would be eliminated. If third parties emerge that are capable of winning at least one state, the failure of either major candidate to get a majority of electoral votes is currently a real possibility (as Chapter 3 demonstrated). Even without third-party candidates, the current system requires the House of Representatives to decide if the two candidates wind up tied in the electoral college as indeed would have happened in 1976 had Ford received 11,950 extra votes in Delaware and Ohio; he and Carter would both have wound up with 269 votes! Direct election, by removing the House of Representatives as a standby decision maker, precludes the possibility of unpredictable House involvement.

There are arguments against direct election,[17] the most compelling of which is that it might result in outcomes where the winner gets far less than a majority of the votes and thus has an insufficient mandate to govern effectively. History suggests, however, that this is not too much of a worry. Only one president, Lincoln, was elected with less than 40 percent of the popular vote; he received 39.8 percent in 1860. And although a good number of presidents have won with under 50 percent, only two presidents (Nixon in 1968 and Wilson in 1912) received less than 45 percent.

Table 6.4
Presidents' Popular Mandate: Two Measures

Year	Winner	Percentage of Popular Vote	Votes Received as Percent of Voting-Age Population*
1952	Eisenhower	55%	34%
1956	Eisenhower	57	34
1960	Kennedy	50	31
1964	Johnson	61	38
1968	Nixon	43	26
1972	Nixon	61	34
1976	Carter	50	27
1980	Reagan	51	27
1984	Reagan	59	31
1988	Bush	53	27

*The figures in this column are based on voting age population estimates made by the Census Bureau.

In any event, the direct election proposals introduced in Congress in 1969 and 1979 provided for a runoff election between the two top candidates in the event that neither got 40 percent of the vote. Some object to this contingency plan on the grounds that it might encourage third parties to try to get sufficient votes to force a runoff that put them in a good bargaining position with the two major parties. But the weight of opinion is that most voters, envisioning votes cast for third parties as throwaway votes, would stick to the major parties, enabling at least one of the candidates to surmount the 40 percent mark and thus obviate the need for a runoff. Moreover, the potential machinations of third parties if a runoff were in the offing pale in comparison with their potential for political skullduggery if neither candidate achieves an electoral college majority under the current rules.

Other objections to direct election can be dismissed quickly. It is said that abolishing the current system would be a blow to federalism.[18] To be sure, state election procedures would require more nationalization to insure that voting qualifications and registration procedures were similar from state to state. But voters from the fifty states would still be considering the interests of their own states (among other things) as they chose among presidential candidates. Moreover, the Congress would continue to be responsive to the concerns of individual states, and the states themselves would lose none of the current powers to act within their own domain.

Some claim that there might be more vote-counting corruption if states lost the special status that the electoral college now affords them, but it is arguable that fraud would be *decreased* under the direct vote plan because it would eliminate the situation where large blocs of electoral votes hinged on how just a few popular votes were distributed. There is conjecture that state and local political parties would be threatened, but they have for years been losing importance in presidential contests increasingly dominated by the national media and the candidates' own organizations. Racial and ethnic minorities point to the advantages they would lose under direct election, but the distribution of benefits and burdens under the electoral college is more complex, as was explained in Chapter 4. Some have worried that noncompetitive states such as those in the South would get too much power if the electoral college were abolished,[19] but this potential impact has been disputed.[20] Besides, justification of the current system based on fears about the probable augmentation or contraction of the power of certain sectors of the electorate under direct election rests on fundamentally undemocratic principles.

The pros of direct election overwhelmingly outweigh the cons. Sweeping away the electoral college sweeps away all of the many problems that have been described in this book. But what is sensible is not always politically feasible; the electoral college is a venerable institution that has resisted change or destruction. Why the electoral college has endured despite uncorrectable flaws, and how the resistance to abolishing it might be overcome, are the topics to which we now turn our attention.

NOTES

1. Quoted in Lawrence Longley and Alan Braun, *The Politics of Electoral College Reform* (New Haven, Conn.: Yale University Press, 1972), pp. 28–29.

2. Quoted in Neal Peirce, *The People's President: The Electoral College in American History and the Direct Vote Alternative* (New York: Simon and Schuster, 1968), p. 181.

3. Longley and Braun, *The Politics of Electoral College Reform*, p. 181.

4. Ibid., p. 54; C. Herman Pritchett, *The American Constitution*, 3d ed. (New York: McGraw-Hill, 1977), p. 255.

5. To deal with the more likely prospect of having to resort to House of Representatives selection, some proportionality proposals introduced in the past would lower the number of electoral votes necessary for election to 40 or 45 percent. But the last time proportionality was introduced in the Congress, the 50 percent electoral vote requirement was maintained.

6. The data presented in this table and in the accompanying text dividing up the 1976 presidential election results by congressional district are for illustration only. They are based on breakdowns of the 1976 vote into the congressional districts of the 1980s (which were the only data available). With reapportionment, the number of representatives in each state changed somewhat, as did district boundaries.

7. See note 6.

8. George Will, "Ready for a New Curriculum at the Electoral College?" *New York Newsday*, June 4, 1990.

9. *Winner Take All: Report of the Twentieth Century Fund Task Force on Reform of the Presidential Election Process* (New York: Holmes and Meier Publishers, 1978).

10. William Keech, "Background Paper," in *Winner Take All*, p. 6.

11. Samuel Merrill, "Empirical Estimates for the Likelihood of a Divided Verdict in a Presidential Election," *Public Choice* 33 (1978), pp. 127–33; Samuel Merrill, "Citizen Voting Power under the Electoral College: A Stochastic Model Based on State Voting Patterns," *SIAM Journal of Applied Mathematics* (March 1978), pp. 376–90. Additional unpublished research on the effects of the national bonus plan done by Merrill was reported by Neal R. Peirce and Lawrence D. Longley, *The People's President: The Electoral College in American History and the Direct Vote Alternative*, rev. ed. (New Haven, Conn.: Yale University Press, 1981), pp. 176–77.

12. Neal Peirce, "A Partial Dissent," in *Winner Take All*, p. 15.

13. Quoted in Congressional Quarterly, *Congressional Quarterly Guide to American Government Fall 79* (Washington, D.C.: Congressional Quarterly, 1979), p. 76.

14. Ibid., p. 74.

15. Ibid., p. 76.

16. For a thorough discussion of nonvoting, see Frances Fox Piven and Richard Cloward, *Why Americans Don't Vote* (New York: Pantheon, 1988).

17. Two books that summarize the objections to the direct election of the president are Judith Best, *The Case Against Direct Election of the President* (Ithaca, N.Y.: Cornell University Press, 1971), and Wallace Sayre and Judith Parris, *Voting for President: The Electoral College and the American Political System* (Washington, D.C.: The Brookings Institution, 1970).

18. Walter Nicgorski, "The New Federalism and Direct Popular Elections," *The Review of Politics* 34 (January 1972), pp. 3–15.

19. Nelson Polsby and Aaron Wildavsky, *Presidential Elections: Strategies of American Electoral Politics*, 2d ed. (New York: Charles Scribner's Sons, 1968), p. 246.

20. Harvey Zeidenstein, "The South Will Not Rise Again through Direct Election of the President, Polsby and Wildavsky Notwithstanding," *Journal of Politics* 31 (August 1969), pp. 808–11.

7

The Politics of Electoral College Abolition

The halls of Congress are strewn with defeated attempts to abolish the electoral college. The first such effort was in 1816; it failed ignominiously, as did dozens of proposals to bring about direct election of the president in the next 150 years. Only in recent years, after a number of elections verged on wrong-winner or no-winner outcomes in the electoral college, did direct election come close to succeeding.

In 1969, a direct election proposal reached the floor of the House of Representatives for the first time since 1826. Never had prospects for discarding of the electoral college looked so good, what with the near-debacle of 1968 and the support of newly elected President Richard Nixon. House Resolution 681, substituting direct vote for the electoral college, passed the House of Representatives by a vote of 338 to seventy, sixty-six votes above the two-thirds necessary for passage of a constitutional amendment. But opponents of direct election in the Senate engaged in a filibuster that proponents could not break, and the amendment failed. Supporters only were able to secure fifty-four votes, well short of the two-thirds necessary to pass an amendment.

This turned out to be the high-water mark of the abolition cause. In 1976 the nation went through another cliff-hanger election; the Ford/Carter race could easily have created a wrong winner (as was shown in Chapter 2). One might think that this close call would have been enough to jolt some reluctant senators into supporting direct election, pushing the Senate vote over the required two-thirds. Not so: Direct election was defeated by an even greater margin in 1979 when the vote was fifty-one to forty-eight, fifteen shy of the number necessary for adoption. Despite over a decade of intense crusading by Senator Birch Bayh and forty-seven days of congressional hearings producing 4,395 pages of testimony, the constitutional change that seems so clearly warranted on the basis of evidence and argument again wound up in the legislative graveyard. The soundness of direct election was insufficient to overcome political realities of the day.

WHY DIRECT ELECTION HAS BEEN DEFEATED

In 1970, ideological considerations caused the defeat of direct election.[1] The old coalition of conservative Republicans and Southern Democrats were the main opponents, seeing direct election as another liberal reform of the same cloth as civil rights and anti-poverty legislation, to which they were also opposed. One way of demonstrating the ideological basis of the vote is to compare the ratings given to supporters and opponents of direct election by the Americans for Democratic Action (ADA), a liberal group that monitors legislative behavior. Those voting for it had an average liberalism score of 65.1; senators who opposed it had a very low score of 14.1. The same cleavage occurred in the House of Representatives, but the more liberal cast of that body enabled the amendment to prevail there.

Battle-lines were drawn a bit differently in 1979, the last time abolition of the electoral college surfaced as an issue in Congress. Even a quick scrutiny of the following roll call shows that voting patterns were more complex.

Democrats for Direct Election (39)

Baucus, Mont.	Gravel, Alaska	Nelson, Wisc.
Bayh, Ind.	Hart, Colo.	Pell, R.I.
Bentsen, Texas	Huddleston, Ky.	Proxmire, Wisc.
Boren, Okla.	Inouye, Hawaii	Pryor, Ark.
Burdick, N.D.	Jackson, Wash.	Randolph, W. Va.
Byrd, W. Va.	Johnston, La.	Ribicoff, Ct.
Church, Idaho	Kennedy, Mass.	Riegle, Mich.
Cranston, Calif.	Leahy, Vt.	Sasser, Tenn.
Culver, Iowa	Levin, Mich.	Stevenson, Ill.
DeConcini, Ariz.	Magnuson, Wash.	Stewart, Ala.
Exon, Neb.	Matsunaga, Hawaii	Tsongas, Mass.
Ford, Ky.	McGovern, S.D.	Williams, N.J.
Glenn, Ohio	Metzenbaum, Ohio	Zorinsky, Neb.

Republicans for Direct Election (12)

Armstrong, Colo.	Danforth, Mo.	Hatfield, Ore.
Baker, Tenn.	Dole, Kansas	Javits, N.Y.
Bellmon, Okla.	Durenberger, Minn.	Mathias, Md.
Chafee, R.I.	Garn, Utah	Stafford, Vt.

Democrats Against Direct Election (20)

Biden, Del.	Eagleton, Mo.	Muskie, Maine
Bradley, N.J.	Heflin, Ala.	Nunn, Ga.
Bumpers, Ark.	Hollings, S.C.	Sarbanes, Md.
Byrd, Va.	Long, La.	Stennis, Mass.
Cannon, Nev.	Melcher, Mont.	Stone, Fla.
Chiles, Fla.	Morgan, N.C.	Talmadge, Ga.
Durkin, N.H.	Moynihan, N.Y.	

Republicans Against Direct Election (28)

Boschwitz, Minn.	Jepsen, Iowa	Schweiker, Pa.
Coichran, Miss.	Kassenbaum, Kansas	Simpson, Wyo.
Cohen, Maine	Laxalt, Nev.	Stevens, Alaska
Domencini, N.M.	Lugar, Ind.	Thurmond, S.C.
Goldwater, Ariz.	McClure, Idaho	Tower, Texas
Hatch, Utah	Percy, Ill.	Wallop, Wyo.
Hayakawa, Calif.	Pressler, S.D.	Warner, Va.
Heinz, Pa.	Roth, Del.	Weicker, Ct.
Helms, N.C.	Schmitt, N.M.	Young, N.D.
Humphrey, N.H.		

The first thing to be noted is that Southerners remained a regional force against direct election. While 73 percent of Southern senators opposed direct election, 58 percent of non-Southern senators favored it. Perhaps this is a die-hard clinging to the "old ways" in a part of the country that continues to be more conservative than the rest of the country. Alternatively, Southern senators might see the electoral college as preserving for the South future opportunities to have leverage in the choice of the president should another Wallace-type candidacy arise creating a situation where neither major party candidate achieves a majority of electoral votes. In any event, the South has continued to be a formidable barrier to direct election.

Whereas Southern resistance to direct election is a bit puzzling, another pattern that emerges from the above roll call is clear-cut and perfectly understandable. As Table 7.1 shows, a large contingent of the opposition to the amendment came from the very small and the very large states, which would stand to lose some power if the electoral college were eliminated.[2] About two-thirds of the senators from the ten smallest states cast negative votes as did a clear majority of those from the ten largest states. As might be expected, senators from the thirty middle-sized states were overwhelmingly supportive.

Table 7.1
Senate Voting on Direct Election, 1979

	For Direct Election	Against Direct Election
10 smallest states	7 (35%)	13 (65%)
10 largest states	9 (45%)	11 (55%)
30 mid-sized states	35 (59%)	24 (41%)

The small state-large state disparity in senatorial voting behavior is even more pronounced if we eliminate the Southerners. As Table 7.2 shows, outside the South support among the mid-sized states was over the two-thirds necessary for passage, but much weaker in the very big states (less than two-thirds) and meager in the tiny states (barely one-third). Clearly, the states that currently have disproportionate power in the electoral college are reluctant to relinquish their power.

We must be careful to qualify the last statement; Tables 7.1 and 7.2 show that other factors affected senators besides the size of their states and whether their states stood to gain or lose from direct election. In fact in twenty-two out of the fifty states the two senators voted in opposite directions: the senators from the largest state (California) were on opposite sides of the fence, and the senators from the smallest state (Alaska) were also divided. Moreover, both senators from the third smallest state (Vermont) were *in favor* of direct election—acting contrary to their state's apparent self-interest. There was considerable idiosyncratic voting, suggesting that for a good number of senators the main factor was what they thought about direct election on the merits of the issue.

Table 7.2
Non-Southern Senators' Voting on Direct Election, 1979

	For Direct Election	Against Direct Election
10 smallest states	7 (35%)	13 (65%)
10 largest states	8 (57%)	6 (43%)
30 mid-sized states	30 (70%)	13 (30%)

One reason that some senators from large states who are usually rather liberal acted otherwise on this issue was the pressure from racial and ethnic minorities who saw *their* influence jeopardized with the demise of the winner-take-all electoral system. Vernon Jordan, president of the National Urban League (a civil rights organization) put the matter bluntly in his congressional testimony against direct election: "Take away the electoral college and the importance of being black melts away. Blacks, instead of being crucial to victory in major states, simply become 10 percent of the total electorate, with reduced impact."[3] When direct election was before the House of Representatives in 1969, two of the three northern Democrats who opposed it were Blacks: William Clay of Missouri and Charles Diggs of Michigan. And in 1979, White senators like Moynihan of New York and Sarbanes of Maryland normally in the forefront of legislation to further democratize American politics were responsive to pleas from Black and Jewish leaders concerned about losing the advantage they thought the electoral college gave them.

Direct election was *not* a burning issue among the public in the 1970s (if ever), nor was it a proposal evoking passionate emotions within the Congress. Some senators were ambivalent, and a number who wound up voting against it could have been swayed. President Nixon in 1970 and President Carter in 1979 might have been able to "twist some arms," using presidential prerogatives to win support from those sitting on the fence. But Nixon was lukewarm about the whole matter (even though it almost cost him the election in 1968) and was apparently angry at Senator Bayh who had been instrumental in the Senate's rejection of two of Nixon's Supreme Court nominees. Carter, who also came perilously close in 1976 to being a "wrong loser," was preoccupied with other matters including fast-moving events in Iran; he too took a backseat role. Lacking effective presidential leadership and mired in somewhat provincial legislative wrangling, direct election fell by the wayside.

FUTURE PROSPECTS

The authors of a painstaking analysis of the 1969–1970 legislative struggle to abolish the electoral college published in 1972 were pessimistic about the chances for change in the absence of the election of a wrong winner.[4] They proved to be prophetic, because the next and last attempt in 1979 to rid the nation of this unwieldy and undemocratic institution was beaten even more decisively. At that point, supporters conceded that any further action was unlikely in the foreseeable future, and the two leading scholars on the electoral college foresaw a "rocky" road for future reform efforts.[5] A substantial contingent of the Congress had gone to war against the electoral college, and the electoral college had won.

Must the nation wait until that inevitable time in the not very distant future when a candidate elected by the people is rejected by the electoral college? Is it necessary for us to have to endure the agony of a president picked through political intrigue in the House of Representatives before our archaic machinery for electing presidents is overhauled? Do the failures to establish direct election in the past presage inevitable defeat if such initiatives are tried again? The answer to these three questions is a tentative no.

There are a number of reasons why prospects for reform might be improved. First, Republicans who have furnished so much of the opposition to direct election may realize that they are the party more likely to be victimized by a wrong-winner outcome. The evidence is now in: Beginning in 1968 a realignment of the electorate took place making the Republicans the dominant party when it comes to electing the president. They have won five out of the six elections between 1968 and 1988, suffering defeat only in 1976, when Carter won because of a backlash against Watergate and because of Southern pride about getting one of their own into the top office. As Chapters 1 and 2 demonstrated, it is now the Republicans whose votes get wasted in the many states where they win handily; the Democrats, where they win at all, win with thin margins of victory. It is a Bush, or a Quayle, or a Dole, who is apt to find himself suffering the fate of a Tilden or a Cleveland of yesteryear—winning the people's vote but losing the Oval Office.

This change in the electorate was not yet clear to observers in 1969 or 1970. Although the Democrats' share of the vote had plummeted eighteen percentage points between 1964, when Lyndon Johnson swept to victory, and 1968, when Nixon won, Nixon barely edged out the Democrat Hubert Humphrey and himself only got 43 percent of the vote. Besides, it was totally unclear how much of that election hinged on temporary disaffection with the Democrats because of the Vietnam War and how much represented waning support for the party generally.

Even by 1979, realignment was doubted and debated. The Watergate scandal had soured many people on the Republicans; the 1976 election had witnessed a resumption to some degree of the old Roosevelt coalition; Democrat Carter *was* president. Who was to know then that a Republican thought by many to be far to the right of the American political mainstream (Reagan) would not only win his party's nomination but twice win the presidency—to be succeeded by his protégé vice president George

Bush? Even the most optimistic of Republicans was not that prescient.

Thus, some Republican senators from small or large states who voted against direct election earlier might now see it *in the interest of their party and hence in their own interest* to change positions even at the expense of having their state lose some slight political advantage. The dividends to a member of Congress and to that member's constituents of having a president of the same party is substantial, probably outweighing a little extra state clout in the electoral college. And those Republicans inclined to vote against direct election simply on the basis of conservative principles might reconsider if (perhaps as a result of reading this book!) they realize that it is Republicans who have the most to gain from abolition.

Another possible change on the political horizon is the behavior of the Southern congressional delegations. The Old South is gone—the South where only Whites voted and where the main issue was keeping Blacks down. In 1989 a Black was elected governor of Virginia, the heart of the Old Confederacy; Blacks today are as likely to vote as Whites; the "Solid South" of old which automatically voted Democratic is long gone; northerners have emigrated to the South in droves. Consequently, it is unlikely that a regional candidate like a Strom Thurmond or a George Wallace could any longer generate sufficient strength to carry states. The days of envisioning some Southern electors as power brokers in a deadlocked electoral college seem to be over, so Southern politicians would seem to have no special interest in holding on to the electoral college status quo.

A more serious obstacle to direct election advocates has been the opposition of part of the Black community. While the massive concentration of Blacks in certain northern states has indubitably given them some additional strength as a result of the winner-take-all rule, this is offset by the plight of Blacks in the South whose votes are generally an exercise in futility. They almost always support the Democratic candidate, who perennially loses in the Southern states. Perhaps Black interest groups and politicians will come to recognize that the enfranchisement of Blacks in the South in the aftermath of the Civil Rights Act of 1965 makes direct election much more compatible with the desire of Blacks to have a major voice in the choosing of the president. Since Blacks now vote with almost the same frequency as Whites and represent 13 percent of the population, they now have the capacity to be a major presence in presidential races on the basis of the sheer number of their votes that are at stake. If Blacks realize that they can be a very effective bloc in a system that puts a premium on a nationwide quest for votes, they might rethink their alliance with conservatives and Southerners to maintain the electoral college.

In the past, the electoral college has won the support of some members of Congress from states with large cities on the grounds that it is a countervailing influence against institutions in the government such as Congress that are biased in favor of rural areas. These lawmakers might now rethink their position since it is currently the suburbs surrounding such cities that seem to hold the balance of power in presidential elections and that gain extra influence as a result of the electoral college. They might also recognize that over the last quarter-century it is Congress that has been one of the forces in American government more responsive to the plight of people living in cities; there is no anti-city bias to redress. Since the pro-urban justification of the electoral college is not applicable in today's political world (whatever merit it once may have had), the opposition of urbanites to direct election may diminish.

Two factors that continue to bolster the direct election forces are the support of a vast array of interest groups and the support of the public. In 1979 a host of civic-minded associations backed the constitutional amendment to eradicate the electoral college, including the American Bar Association, the League of Women Voters, the American Civil Liberties Association, and Common Cause. In addition, a strange coalition of partisan groups came together in support of changing the Constitution, among which were the U.S. Chamber of Commerce and the AFL-CIO, who are normally at each others' throats. There is no reason to suppose that this amalgam of interests would abandon their support for direct election.

The public has no particular fondness for the electoral college. Since 1966, Gallup polls have routinely found that about two-thirds of those interviewed favor direct election.[6] This squares with a poll of state legislators back in 1966 showing 59 percent in favor of ending the electoral college,[7] an impressive finding since these politicians have vested interests in staying in touch with public sentiment. These data are important for two reasons: They suggest that representatives and senators will not suffer politically if they support direct election, and they augur well for ratification of a constitutional amendment that requires the approval of the legislatures of three-fourths of the states.

Thus, the chances for abolition of the electoral college may not be as gloomy as they seemed a decade ago. The possibility that some Republicans might move to the forefront of the movement for reform in light of their party's dominance in presidential elections, the transformation of the South, and the persistence of a sympathetic climate of opinion provide some hope that the logjam preventing direct election can be broken before a political debacle takes place.

What is necessary now is the exercise of leadership, the emergence of some national political figure willing to take up where Senator Birch Bayh left off to resume the battle against the electoral college. To be sure, this is a cause unlikely to generate much passion in the absence of a wrong winner debacle or near-debacle. But it is an issue that deserves to be placed once again on the nation's political agenda.

NOTES

1. Lawrence Longley and Alan Braun, *The Politics of Electoral College Reform* (New Haven, Conn.: Yale University Press, 1972), chap. 5.

2. Research done in 1979 by Joseph Gorman for the Congressional Research Service confirmed the results of earlier work on the relationship

between state size and electoral college biases. Gorman concluded that "the present system gives a significant advantage to the most populous states, a smaller advantage to the less populous states, and disadvantages to the greatest extent the medium-sized states, having between 4 and 12 electoral votes, which are too large to benefit to any significant degree from the 'constant two' but are too small to derive significant benefit from the general ticket system." Joseph Gorman, Memorandum to Senator Birch Bayh, March 12, 1979, in U.S. Congress, Senate, Senate Judiciary Committee, Subcommittee on the Constitution, *Hearings on Direct Popular Election of the President and Vice-President of the U.S.*, 96 Cong., 1st session, March 27 and 30, and April 3 and 9, 1979, pp. 49–50.

3. Quoted in Congressional Quarterly, *Congressional Quarterly Guide to American Government 79* (Washington, D.C.: Congressional Quarterly, 1979), p. 78.

4. Longley and Braun, *The Politics of Electoral College Reform*, pp. 177–78.

5. Neal Peirce and Alan Longley, *The People's President: The Electoral College in American History and the Direct Vote Alternative*, rev. ed. (New Haven, Conn.: Yale University Press, 1981), p. 206.

6. "2 out of 3 in Poll Favor Ending Electoral College," The *New York Times*, December 4, 1980, p. A26.

7. Cited in Neal R. Peirce, *The People's President: The Electoral College in American History and the Direct Vote Alternative* (New York: Simon and Schuster, 1968), p. 206.

Epilogue: A Plea for Democracy

When our Constitution was adopted, democracy was a newborn and much doubted ideal. James Madison, one of the major architects, was very skeptical about giving power to the majority. In his classic essay *"The Federalist, No. 10,"* he argued in favor of putting major constraints on the role of the people in the government.

This fear of the populace permeated the Constitution. Federal judges were to be appointed; the United States Senate was to be selected by the state legislatures rather than the people; states were left free to exclude all kinds of people from voting. The electoral college that kept the people at arm's length from the selection of the president was in keeping with this elitist conception of government.

But early on in our history, democratic impulses took over. Little by little, the right to vote was extended—to those without property, to non-Christians, to Blacks, and to women. Together with gradual enfranchisement came the extension of popular elections, including the Seventeenth Amendment, ratified in 1913, which provided for direct election of the Senate. Other devices instituted around the turn of the century in many states to give people more control over government were the recall, the referendum, and the initiative. Democratic governance has been further extended in the contemporary era: Legislatures have been reapportioned on a one person-one vote basis; poll taxes were eliminated by the Twenty-Fourth Amendment; civil rights laws have been passed providing federal machinery to register those long excluded from voting; citizens in the District of Columbia were given the right to vote for president. Democratization has been a hallmark of American political development.

The electoral college remains curiously out of step with these democratic developments, a relic of a bygone age when it was thought proper to limit the role of the people. We elect senators, governors, mayors, and all kinds of other officials through a simple process: The candidate who gets the most votes wins. Direct election of officials, without intermediaries, is the norm throughout the United States—except for the most important office in the land. It is time to remove this glaring inconsistency from the framework of American government and make the presidency a truly democratic institution.

Some eminent scholars have disagreed with this notion. Yale University Law School professor Alexander Bickel as recently as 1971 condemned the concept of direct election as a device for stripping minority groups of power. His vision of democracy is one of countervailing powers, and he sees the electoral college as aiding certain interests that are shortchanged elsewhere in the political system. Says Bickel: "Practical men interested in perfecting the American democracy should disenthrall themselves from the romance of pure majoritarianism."[1]

We emphatically disagree. It is not romance to let majority vote determine who wins elective offices; it is the very essence of democracy. There is simply no other valid way of putting into practice the noble idea that every person should have an equal opportunity to determine who runs the government. The Supreme Court of the United States has made the point well: "The conception of political equality from the Declaration of Independence, to Lincoln's Gettysburg Address, to the Fifteenth, Seventeenth, and Nineteenth Amendments can mean only one thing—one person, one vote."[2]

The above postulate was applied as a justification for striking down an indirect primary system in Georgia whereby counties cast votes as a unit depending on which candidate won in the particular county. The principle is just as applicable as a condemnation of the electoral college, which makes some people's vote worth more than others, and which makes the people's votes subsidiary to a body that very poorly represents people's choices. In the Gettysburg Address Lincoln poignantly spoke about saving the "government of the people, by the people, and for the people." For that vision to become a reality, we need a president "of the people, by the people, and for the people." Abolishing the electoral college and letting the people decide who should be president would be a giant step in that direction. In the United States, direct election of the president is a sine qua non of democracy.

In the final analysis, partisan interests need to be disregarded in assessing the electoral college. It doesn't matter whether it is the Democrats or Republicans who benefit. It doesn't matter that big states and small states gain from it. It doesn't matter how it affects Blacks, Jews, or Mormons. It doesn't matter whether cities, suburbs, or rural areas get an edge. It doesn't matter whether third parties are advantaged or disadvantaged. It doesn't matter if the presidency is strengthened or weakened by the electoral college.

What matters is that the electoral college is morally wrong. It is undemocratic and therefore indefensible. Wrong winners, House of Representative mischief, and unfair allocation of electors have no place in our political system. We should let the people's votes decide who the president will be, letting the chips fall where they may. The preferred choice of the greatest number of people, for better or worse, should be president of the United States.

NOTES

1. Alexander Bickel, *Reform and Continuity: The Electoral College, the Convention, and the Party System* (New York: Harper and Row, 1971), p. 17.

2. *Gray v. Sanders*, 372 U.S. 368 (1963).

Selected Bibliography

BOOKS

Best, Judith. *The Case Against Direct Election of the President*. Ithaca, N.Y.: Cornell University Press, 1971.

Bickel, Alexander. *Reform and Continuity: The Electoral College, the Convention, and the Party System*. New York: Harper and Row, 1971.

Brams, Steven. *The Presidential Election Game*. New Haven, Conn.: Yale University Press, 1978.

Diamond, Martin. *The Electoral College and the American Idea of Democracy*. Washington, D.C.: American Enterprise Institute, 1977.

Longley, Lawrence, and Alan Braun. *The Politics of Electoral College Reform*. New Haven, Conn.: Yale University Press, 1972.

Matthews, Donald, ed. *Perspectives on Presidential Selection*. Washington, D.C.: Brookings Institution, 1973.

Michener, James. *Presidential Lottery: The Reckless Gamble in Our Election System*. New York: Random House, 1969.

Nelson, Michael, ed. *The Elections of 1988*. Washington, D.C.: Congressional Quarterly, 1989.

Peirce, Neal R. *The People's President: The Electoral College in American History and the Direct Vote Alternative* (New York: Simon and Schuster, 1968).

Peirce, Neal R, and Lawrence D. Longley. *The People's President: The Electoral College in American History and the Direct Vote Alternative*, rev. ed. New Haven, Conn.: Yale University Press, 1981.

Polsby, Nelson, and Aaron Wildavsky. *Presidential Elections: Strategies of American Electoral Politics*, 2d ed. New York: Charles Scribner's Sons, 1968.

Pomper, Gerald, et al. *The Election of 1988: Reports and Interpretations*. Chatham, N.J.: Chatham House Publishers, 1989.

Sayre, Wallace, and Judith Parris. *Voting for President: The Electoral College and the American Political System*. Washington, D.C.: The Brookings Institution, 1970.

Winner Take All: Report of the Twentieth Century Fund Task Force on Reform of the Presidential Election Process. New York: Holmes and Meier Publishers, 1978.

Zeidenstein, Harvey. *Direct Election of the President*. Lexington, Mass.: D. C. Heath, 1973.

ARTICLES

Arrington, Theodore S., and Saul Brenner. "Should the Electoral College Be Replaced by the Direct Election of the President? A Debate," *P.S.* 17 (Spring 1984), pp. 237–50.

Banzhaf, John F., III. "One Man, 3312 Votes: A Mathematical Analysis of the Electoral College," *Villanova Law Review*, 13 (Winter 1968), pp. 303–46.

Brams, Steven. "The 3/2s Rule in Presidential Campaigning," *American Political Science Review* 68 (March 1974), pp. 113–34.

Longley, Lawrence D., and James D. Dana. "New Empirical Estimates of the Electoral College for the 1980s," *Western Political Quarterly* 37 (March 1984), pp. 157–75.

Nelson, Michael. "Partisan Bias in the Electoral College," *Journal of Politics* 36 (November 1974), pp. 1033–48.

Nicgorski, Walter. "The New Federalism and Direct Popular Election," *The Review of Politics* 34 (January 1972), pp. 3–15.

Pomper, Gerald. "The Southern 'Free Elector' Plan," *The Southwestern Social Science Quarterly* 45 (June 1964), pp. 16–24.

Rabinowitz, George, and Stuart Elaine MacDonald. "The Power of the States in U.S. Presidential Elections," *American Political Science Review* 80 (March 1985), pp. 65–87.

Smith, Eric R. A. N., and Peverill Squire. "Direct Election of the President and the Power of the States," *Western Political Quarterly* 40 (March 1987), pp. 29–44.

Spilerman, Seymour, and David Dickens, "Who Will Gain and Who Will Lose Influence under Different Electoral Rules," *American Journal of Sociology* 80 (September 1974), pp. 443–77.

Sterling, Carleton. "Electoral College Biases Revealed: The Conventional Wisdom and Game Theory Models Notwithstanding," *Western Political Quarterly* 31 (June 1978), pp. 159–77.

Yunker, John, and Lawrence Longley. "The Electoral College: Its Biases Newly Measured for the 1960's and 1970's," *American Politics Series in Sage Professional Papers*. Beverly Hills, Calif.: Sage Publications, 1976.

Index

ABOUT THE AUTHORS

DAVID W. ABBOTT is an associate professor of political science at Brooklyn College of the City University of New York. He has taught, researched, and written about American politics for twenty-five years. His publications include two editions of a widely used reader on American political parties. A practitioner of survey research, Abbott has conducted numerous survey studies in the field of politics and public opinion.

JAMES P. LEVINE is a professor of political science at Brooklyn College and the Graduate Center of the City University of New York. He has written many articles on the judicial process, has co-authored two books on criminal justice, and is the author of a forthcoming book entitled *Juries and Politics*. Levine has also regularly taught American politics and has published several articles in this field.